OLTMANS

A MOMENT IN HISTORY

TOMMY WILKENS &
HILDE WILKENS VANRENTERGHEM

Dedication

We dedicate our book to the late Willem Oltmans, in honor of his body of work. Without his tenacity and drive to become a first-class journalist and his lifelong commitment to recording the details of his life in his personal diaries, we could not have brought this intriguing story to light.

Willem Oltmans

~ **Tommy Wilkens & Hilde Wilkens Vanrenterghem**

TABLE OF CONTENTS

PREFACE

We would like to express our greatest appreciation for the guidance and encouragement provided by our late friend and fellow researcher/author/poet Paul Foreman of Austin, Texas. It helped to make this work possible.

We also want to thank Dr. Ad Leerinvelt, the Curator of Modern Day Manuscripts of The Dutch Royal Library in Den Haag, The Netherlands.

We thank Steven Martin for sharing with us his memories of the real Marguerite Oswald and allowing us to include them here. And we appreciate the efforts of our editor, Ken Dixon.

Finally, we would like to thank you for choosing to read our book and take a closer second look at the late Willem Oltmans' life, his investigation into President John F. Kennedy's assassination and his close friendship with **George de Mohrenschildt.**

INTRODUCTION

In this book, we'll tell the fascinating true story of Dutch journalist Willem Oltmans and his ten-year intimate friendship with Baron George de Mohrenschildt, who was - by all known accounts - the closest friend of Lee Harvey Oswald in the months leading up to the assassination of President John F. Kennedy.

Oltmans published his own book on this subject years ago, but it was largely ignored. Now, upon completion of our in-depth study of the Willem Oltmans archive in Den Haag, The Netherlands, we're able to offer the reader a very well-researched second look at his findings.

OLTMANS: *A Moment In History* won't reveal who fired the shots that killed President Kennedy. But it does shed new light on the connection between Oswald and one of the most mysterious individuals known to have been associated with him.

The Oltmans archive contains literally thousands of pages in bound, diary-type binders. It includes hand-written letters, notes and pictures related to both his journalistic work and his personal life. It is through his eyes and his investigative prowess that this story comes alive.

The records have been stored and preserved under the watchful eye of Dr. Ad Leerinvelt, Curator of Modern Day Manuscripts at the Dutch Royal Library in Den Haag. Among them, we discovered a wealth of startling information regarding the private lives of George and Jeanne de Mohrenschildt – details that until now have not been made public.

What Willem Oltman's ten-year-long investigation uncovered concerning George de Mohrenschildt and his self-confessed involvement with Lee Harvey Oswald led to the journalist being conspired against and discredited by representatives of the Dutch Government. Both his character and his findings were called into question. And certain elements of the American mainstream media followed suit. But a careful analysis of the facts confirms that, as an investigative journalist, Oltmans was both diligent and honest in his pursuit of the truth.

We begin on June 6, 1925, in Huizen, The Netherlands, with the birth of Willem Leonard Oltmans to Antonie Cornelis Oltmans and Alexandrine van der Woude. His father had been born on June 24, 1894, in Central Java, Indonesia, and became a respected and admired chemical engineer. Later, he achieved further success as an attorney-at-law.

Alexandrine van der Woude was born on June 21, 1896, in Maarsen, The Netherlands. She was educated in both classic languages and science and received violin training in Liege, Belgium.

The Oltmans family had amassed considerable wealth through investments in the production of quinine in the Dutch West Indies. Records show that Willem Oltmans was schooled at some of The Netherlands' most prestigious educational institutions in his early years. Growing up in Huis ter Heide at "De Horst", the family villa, he enjoyed a carefree lifestyle available to only the wealthiest and most elite.

But, even with these advantages, Oltmans told of struggling in childhood with loneliness and the belief that no one ever understood his feelings or accepted him as he was. He was devastated by the thought that he had not lived up to the expectations of his parents, and he would spend the rest of his life estranged from them.

It was at age nine that Willem Oltmans began keeping a diary. Having no meaningful relationship with others, he was driven to record his deepest and most private thoughts. It was the start of a discipline of daily note-taking that would continue throughout his life. His motive was to establish a work that showed how a human develops over time. He viewed writing as an accomplishment in and of itself, and his diaries and later publications became, as it were, his *raison d'etre*.

It's in his observations that we're able to see not only the inner thoughts of the man himself but the process by which he gathers and analyzes information. And it's this meticulous approach that lends credence to his recounting of the de Mohrenschildt/Oswald relationship.

Formal education would prove to be difficult and frustrating for young Oltmans. After failing at one school after another, in 1946 he was accepted at the Dutch Education Institute for Foreign Countries in Castle "Nijenrode" in Beukelen. But feeling overwhelmed once again by his studies, he dropped out and returned home defeated.

By 1948, however, Oltmans had regrouped and made a life-changing decision. He ventured to America and enrolled at prestigious Yale University to study Political Science. That bold move, unfortunately, ended in failure. And having to drop out of Yale sent him into a deep depression.

He returned home to The Netherlands feeling more alone and misunderstood than ever. At this same time, his diary entries indicate, Oltmans was in the throes of a personal identity crisis that was closely tied to his innermost secret: his strong homosexual tendencies and the fear that they might be revealed. It was a battle he would fight within himself throughout his life.

In denial regarding his true feelings, he met and fell in love with Josephine Anna Frederick Westerman in 1950. And five years later, they were engaged to be married. She was the daughter of an Esso Oil and Gas Company executive and worked as a ground stewardess for KLM Airlines. Their wedding took place on December 19, 1957, in New York City. But the marriage was short-lived and ended with a divorce trial, where evidence was presented that his wife had caught Oltmans in bed with a male companion.

A move to Rome after the divorce proved to be the catalyst for what would become a very successful career in journalism. Beginning in the earliest weeks of his work as a freelance correspondent for several of the city's newspapers, Oltmans established his credo that a search for the facts must guide anything that he covered. He soon earned his reputation as a reporter who would never compromise the truth, and it was his unyielding professional standards that led him to uncover some of the biggest stories around the world.

The life of a globetrotting reporter suited Oltmans well. Traveling from one big story to the next soon earned him the nickname "The Flying Dutchman". Having finally discovered his niche in life, he found that his competence and charisma led him to almost instant success. He never shied away from danger and found his way to information in places where his contemporaries were afraid to go.

Oltmans' strong drive and commitment to becoming a world-class investigative reporter would afford him opportunities that others could only envy. It was perhaps inevitable that his methods created a stir on many fronts, and he soon had the reputation of being The Netherlands' most controversial and radical journalist.

In 1956, he was doing correspondence work for <u>De Telegraaf,</u> a morning newspaper located in Amsterdam, The Netherlands, with a circulation of nearly half a million readers per day. At that time, the government and Indonesia were engaged in a contentious dispute over the rightful ownership of Dutch New Guinea. Instructions were passed down to Oltmans from the publishers of <u>De Telegraaf</u> not to interview Indonesian President Kusno Achmed Sukarno or in any other way involve himself in the situation.

But Oltmans openly expressed his belief that Indonesia did in fact have rights to the territory. Furthermore, he defied the publishers' orders by not only meeting with Sukarno but soon becoming the President's close friend and confidant. Entries in his diaries reveal that the relationship was physically intimate as well – and that Sukarno's wife was aware of it, although she didn't approve and hated to see Oltmans arrive for a visit.

The meeting with President Sukarno was reported by the <u>Elseviers Weekblad</u> (Elseviers Weekly Paper) and made headlines all over The Netherlands and around Europe. Understandably, <u>De Telegraaf</u> not only fired Oltmans but refused to publish any story he might write in the future. The newspaper's far-reaching influence on the Continent would affect him for many years. And the Dutch Minister of Foreign Affairs, Joseph Luns, organized a covert smear campaign to cast doubt upon and discredit and ruin Willem Oltmans.

Joseph Luns

What had he done to generate such animosity at the highest levels of government? President Sukarno believed deeply that Dutch New Guinea belonged rightfully to Indonesia and was ready to mobilize his country's army and take back the territory by force if needed. With tempers boiling on both sides, it was Oltmans who had stepped into the controversy and sent then-President John F. Kennedy a private message through his closest international advisers – one that is widely believed to have averted war. It's thought that Oltmans asked President Kennedy to apply pressure to the Dutch Government to turn over the territory to a temporary United Nations Administration (UNTEA).

He then aligned himself with an informal group of business leaders who circumvented the authorities and worked to convince the Dutch public that the Government should relinquish Dutch New Guinea to Indonesia. Luns was so infuriated by Oltmans' actions that he gave direct instructions to avoid the journalist and never to publish anything with his byline from that moment on (calling him "one motorized mosquito"). This boycott and blacklisting of Willem Oltmans would remain in place for several decades.

On May 1, 1963, Indonesia took control of Dutch New Guinea. And Oltmans' involvement in the efforts leading to this momentous event had earned him some very dangerous enemies inside the Dutch Government. Soon, his phone stopped ringing. The once shining star of Dutch journalism was now being shunned and ridiculed and - worst of all for a reporter - his honesty and integrity were called into question at every turn. It was an attack on the very qualities that had defined his career and upon which he had built his reputation.

Oltmans' notes reveal his certainty that someone within the Dutch government was behind the move to ruin him both personally and professionally. However, it would take many years for him to unearth the facts that proved his case. And during that time, he lived in near poverty and was even forced to collect welfare in order to support a somewhat normal existence. Oltmans worked as a freelance journalist who reported on and sold small stories to whatever publications would pay him the most. It was a hard life, and the paydays were small and far-between. But his vindication was to come.

By 1991, Oltmans had filed a lawsuit against the Dutch State Government, which included the Royal Family. There was a long, drawn-out legal battle, and a settlement was reached nine years later. The defendants were found liable, and through binding arbitration the Dutch State was ordered to pay Willem Oltmans eight million guilders ($4,469,273.76 in 2000). About a quarter of that amount was required to cover his legal fees.

Despite those many years of struggle, he never lost his determination to work at what he knew he did best: reporting stories and being a journalist. It was a long and difficult climb, but he struggled back up the ladder and ultimately reached a level of success.

For income in the 1960s, Oltmans turned to the lecture circuits in Europe and as far away as the United States. He worked for the Keedick Lecture Bureau at one point and earned $100 to $125 per lecture. His talks were mainly given to women's groups and civic organizations. In addition to the pay, the cost of airfare, transportation to and from the airport and a guaranteed meal were included. It was work on a small scale, but he was glad to have it and it payed the bills. And it's how he became involved in investigating the killing of John F. Kennedy.

CHAPTER ONE

The date was March 8, 1964, and Willem Oltmans had just finished presenting a lecture at the Criterion Club of Wichita Springs, Texas. After a short commuter flight back to the Dallas-Fort Worth Airport, he was awaiting his departure to New York when he spotted 55-year-old Marguerite Oswald, mother of accused assassin Lee Harvey Oswald.

In his personal notes, he described her as a disheveled-looking middle-aged woman struggling with her luggage, which consisted of a broken suitcase and multiple cardboard boxes. Seeing the possibility of a story, Oltmans approached Mrs. Oswald and asked if he could be of assistance.

"How do you know me?" she asked. His reply was, "The whole world knows you." The two began a short conversation, during which he discovered that they would both be traveling on American Airlines Flight 25 to the recently renamed John F. Kennedy International Airport.

She was on her way to sell sixteen handwritten letters that Lee had sent to her while he was living in Russia. Esquire magazine would be buying them for $4000. She had signed and dated each one and included a small notation, as if to add a personal touch.

In his notes, Oltmans describes Marguerite Oswald as a worn out and deeply-stressed woman with dark, inset eyes, wearing dark-rimmed cat's-eye glasses and a look of helplessness and despair. She was a picture of total sadness. But her mind seemed to be moving at a thousand miles an hour, and it never stopped during the entire trip to New York.

Soon after they settled into seats 7E and 7F on the plane, she began a asking series of what he characterized as "questions on top of questions".

Why had her son not been given legal counsel on that Friday afternoon or evening, nor the entire day Saturday, nor all the way until he was shot dead in the Dallas Municipal Building? If he had been wealthy, might he be alive today?

Was my son denied the right to a lawyer because he had no money? Why was no recording ever made of the more than twenty hours of interrogation that had been done between Friday afternoon and Sunday morning? Why were no notes ever taken? Her son was accused of murdering the President of The United States, and no notes were taken and a recording wasn't made. It just didn't seem right. Something was fishy.

Lee had steadfastly denied again and again shooting anyone, from his arrest on Friday afternoon all the way until he was murdered in handcuffs. She said she had been allowed to meet with him at the jail on Saturday, and "he looked me straight in the eyes and said, 'Momma, don't worry. I did not murder anybody, not the police officer or no one, and this will all be cleared up'".

In Oltmans' notes, he tells of asking Marguerite Oswald if it was at all possible that her son could have killed President Kennedy. And Mrs. Oswald replied that there was a chance that he had. "But until it is proven in our United States court system, I will fight for my son's rights and I will never believe that he did kill the President," she said. "My son is dead and he can not defend himself, so as his mother I will defend him to the last stand.

In my testimony before the Warren Commission in Washington, I asked Chief Justice Warren why wasn't there a recording of my son's interrogation on that Friday and Saturday, being that he was accused of such a horrible crime?"

Chief Justice Warren couldn't provide an answer, but he did pose the same question to Dallas Police Chief Jesse Curry. The response was, "Well, we were going to buy a recorder for important cases. We talked about getting one, but we just never got around to it." In an awkwardly quiet moment in the hearing room, everyone wondered how could that have happened.

She spoke of of the day of Lee's funeral and how even in death there was no peace or respect for her murdered son, killed while in custody and - even worse - handcuffed to a policeman. Rose Hill Memorial Cemetery, at 7301 East Lancaster Avenue in Fort Worth, was the only one in the entire metropolitan area that would accept Lee Oswald for burial.

There were eight Dallas police officers, two guard dogs and a few news people in attendance. A small prayer service had been planned for four o'clock in the chapel, but that was halted before it could begin. The family was heartbroken. How could this be happening? Events had moved so quickly from Friday to Monday that it was all a blur in their minds.

Now it was time to bury Lee and each of them would begin what would be a lifetime of soul-searching and wondering what had really happened. Bitterness and hatred followed them all like a pitch-black shadow. Even half a century later, the name "Oswald" would evoke horrible memories in the mind of anyone who had lived through those traumatic days.

The Oswald casket was a #31 Pine Bluff model, made from cheap wood. Records would reveal that Robert Oswald, brother of the deceased, had purchased it on November 24,1963, from the Miller Funeral Home of Tarrant County, Texas, for $300.

Preston McGraw of United Press International said, "Well, if we're going to write a story of this son-of-a-bitch's funeral, we're going to have to carry him out of here."

Seven newsmen, including Jerry Flemmons of the Fort Worth Star-Telegram and Mike Cochran from Associated Press, took hold of the handles and moved the body with some difficulty to the freshly-dug grave.

Oswald pallbearers

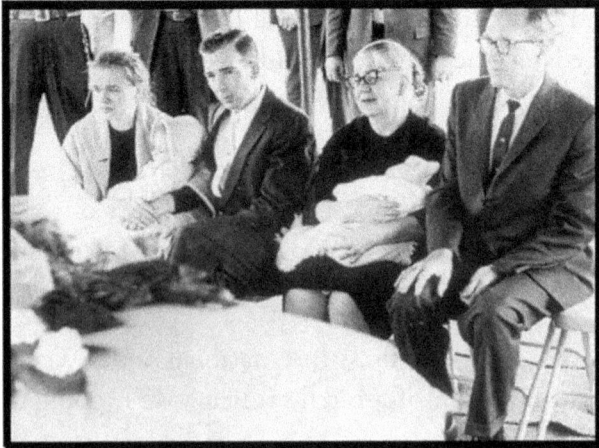

Oswald family at funeral

With no minister present, there wasn't much left to do but proceed with the burial. The grave diggers had been told that they were preparing the site for a man named William Bobo, an old Texas cowboy from a time gone by. As the family members sat close to the casket and consoled one another, just moments before the coffin was to be lowered into the ground, a dark sedan pulled into the parking area.

Listening to his car radio, the Reverend Louis A. Saunders, Executive Secretary of the local Council of Churches, had heard that Lee Oswald was to be buried in the Rose Hill Cemetery and later told of his feeling that something just wasn't right. He drove to the cemetery. The Oswald family had arranged for two Lutheran ministers to conduct the funeral service, but both had backed out at the last minute, citing real fear for their own safety. Hatred and bitterness had gripped Dallas.

In keeping with his faith, Reverend Saunders stepped forward. With no Bible in hand, he conducted a short but heartfelt funeral service entirely from memory. He recited the 23d Psalm: "The Lord is my shepherd, I shall not be in want. He makes me lie down in green pastures, he leads me beside quiet waters, he restores my soul. He guides me in paths of righteousness for his name's sake. Even though I walk through the valley of the shadow of death, I will fear no evil, for you are with me; your rod and your staff, they comfort me.

You prepare a table before me in the presence of my enemies. You anoint my head with oil; my cup overflows. Surely goodness and love will follow me all the days of my life, and I will dwell in the house of the LORD forever." And a passage from John 14: "Do not let your hearts be troubled. Trust in God; trust also in me. In my Father's house are many rooms; if it were not so, I would have told you. I am going there to prepare a place for you. And if I go and prepare a place for you, I will come back and take you to be with me that you also may be where I am. You know the way to the place where I am going."

And so, in the final seconds, Lee Oswald would have a funeral service after all. It provided some comfort to the grief-stricken family. At 4:28 P. M., the casket was interred. The Oswald family had lost a son, a brother, a husband and a father. There, on the western most edge of Rose Hill Cemetery, in the section called Sunset 18, Lee Oswald 's simple grave was all that remained. But, despite the pain and sorrow that the nation and the entire world had endured since those horrible few seconds on that Friday afternoon, there had still been a small place for forgiveness and prayer, thanks to one minister's act of kindness.

There were two funerals on that chilly November day in 1963. The one right outside of Washington, DC, a somber ceremony for a leader who had brought hope and change not only to the citizens of the United States but to people around the world, held everyone's attention. And on that small patch of earth in sun-baked Texas, one grave stood out, with its plain and simple headstone showing just a name and no dates. And within it lay secrets now buried for all eternity.

Lee Harvey Oswald grave marker

Years later, Saunders would express his regrets at having been there, saying, "I wish it could have been taken care of in a different way. But the whole experience deepened my conviction that the Christian faith has a redeeming, saving and reconciling work to say for every living being. It reinforced my awareness that God's love is not confined to the so-called good people." He was a native of Richlands, N.C., and a graduate of Johnson Bible College in Tennessee. Later, he studied theology at Duke University and received his divinity degree from Vanderbilt University. Until his death on April 5, 1998, Saunders remained a dedicated Christian minister.

It was these first-hand accounts, rich with detail, from Marguerite Oswald that led Oltmans to realize that he had a story that should be told - how the hardships of raising three young sons by herself affected an already poor and struggling mother who, at times, worked two jobs just to make ends meet, how a woman who, after being thrust into the middle of a nightmare event with no end in sight, could still hold her head high and tell everyone who would listen of her deep belief that her child was innocent. When they arrived in New York, he arranged a return trip to Dallas the following day to talk with her again.

CHAPTER TWO

Oltman's notes regarding his arrival at Marguerite Oswald's home tell of a small and tidy house, no different from thousands of others in America. Her living room walls were covered with family pictures – testament to a time when life was kinder and more gentle but still filled with struggle and hard work. Hardship was really all her small family had ever known. As the two sat down together, she began to reminisce about her late son.

"You know, Lee's father died two months before he was even born. I was married for the second time on July 20, 1933, to Robert Edward Lee Oswald. We were married in the Lutheran Church. He was a good man. He worked as a insurance premium collector for the Metropolitan Life Insurance Company of New Orleans. It was hard times in those days, and people were poor. Robert would come home with the saddest stories of people's lives.

"I'll never forget that day when Robert died in our front yard on Alvar Street. I remember it was a hot day in New Orleans, even though it was October. Robert was out in the front yard mowing the grass and just all of a sudden dropped to the ground. He had a heart attack right there in the front yard. We had argued earlier in the day and I guess it went on for several hours. I don't even remember what we argued about now. I guess our marriage was kind of shaky. But now, when I think back, it was the happiest time of my whole life.

"It was hard times on us back then, and Robert had even mentioned divorce as we argued. I was just plain mad and upset, and then Robert dropped dead. I was seven months pregnant with Lee and all alone again. I felt bad over the years. I had Robert buried the very same day he died.

I guess his family never got over that nor spoke to me again. My son Lee was born on October 18, 1939. I gave him his first name Lee after his father, and his middle name Harvey came from his paternal grandmother's maiden name.

"It's hard to even explain the hardships in those days. I had three young boys and the responsibilities, being the only parent, were just almost unbearable. After a move to 1010 Bartholomew Street, I opened a small store in the front room of our house and called it 'Oswald 's Notion Shop'. We struggled, but I was determined to have a normal family. We even had a pet dog named 'Sunshine'. But finally it all became too much, and I could not do it all alone.

"I was forced, for financial reasons, on January 3, 1942, to apply for admission to the Evangelical Lutheran Bethlehem Orphan Asylum Association to place my two oldest boys, John and Robert, in the Bethlehem Children's Home. Due to his young age, Lee was denied entry. After I reapplied for Lee's admittance, he was accepted on the day after Christmas - December 26, 1942 - with the understanding that $10 per month would be paid to the children 's home to help with clothing and other needed items. Regular visits to see all three boys were arranged and weekend outings were common.

"Over the years I have been degraded, belittled and humiliated over making that decision. At the time I could not support and raise the three all alone. I placed the boys in the Lutheran-run home because I felt deep down it was the best for the boys. In spite of what all has been written and said about me, I only wanted what was best for my children. As time moved on, things did get somewhat better and I was able to get all three of my sons back home and living with me. We did move around a lot, but in those days I had to go where the jobs were and where we could find affordable housing.

"In the summer of 1943, I met a man originally from Boston named Edwin Ekdahl. He was an electrical engineer by trade who had a substantial income.

Edwin Ekdahl and Marguerite Oswald

"After a short courtship, we were married in May of 1945. This would be my third marriage. We moved to Benbrook, Texas, on Granbury Road. All three boys got along well with their stepfather, but most of all Lee admired and looked up to Edwin.

"For the first time in his whole life, Lee had a father figure. The two just got along so well together just like a real father and son would. I knew that's what Lee needed so badly. He was the youngest of my three boys, and sometimes I felt he needed a little something more...a little more attention. And Edwin gave him that.

"But it was a short-lived marriage because of Edwin's infidelities. I finally just had enough of his repeated lies about seeing another woman, so I set out to show him I knew just what he was up to. One day, my oldest son John and myself followed Edwin several streets over from our home. We watched him stop and park his car and go into a house. I had John go to the door and knock, as if he was a telegram delivery boy. When the lady opened the door I rushed in from the side and there sat Edwin in his shorts and a t-shirt and the woman was dressed in a negligee. The look on his face!

"From that moment on, the marriage was filled with bitterness and fighting on an almost daily basis. The marriage was over and had not lasted a full year. Edwin was stingy, and the frequent arguments about his insistence that I account for my expenditures just fueled the resentment. After several attempts to reconcile and salvage the marriage and a move to Covington, Louisiana, at 311 Vermont Street, the marriage was broken with no hope. Finally in March of 1948, Edwin was granted a divorce decree. The trial showed 'excesses, harsh and cruel treatment and outrages' toward Edwin.

"As I look back now, I sometimes wonder how we made it, with the struggle and the hardships and what seemed like at times always being down and out. But I can honestly say we were never trash. We moved to Benbrook, Texas, on San Saba Street. We did the best we could do. My two oldest boys, John and Robert, had joined the military. John joined the United States Coast Guard and then transferred into the United States Air Force. Robert joined the United States Marine Corps on July 11, 1952.

"Lee just looked up to them so much and talked of when he could join. Even at sixteen, he wanted to become a United States Marine. Of course I said no. It stopped him from joining, but it didn't slow his desire to be a Marine. Lee would study the Marine manual till he knew that book inside and out. It was during this period that Lee went by the nickname 'Yankee'.

"It was so disappointing to me that Lee had only made it to the tenth grade. Once I had moved with Lee to Fort Worth, he enrolled at Arlington Heights High School. It didn't last. On October 24, 1956, Lee enlisted in the United States Marine Corps, just days after his seventeenth birthday. I was such a proud mother. Lee was so proud and he finally had what he had so longed for.

"I have never been able to pinpoint it, but once Lee had been in the Marine Corps for a time, there was a clear, noticeable change in my son. He just acted strange, it seemed, and was so very secretive. Once he had left the Marine Corps and gone to Russia, I was just sure as a mother who knows her son that Lee was some sort of an agent."

Lee Harvey Oswald

Upon hearing this, Oltmans asked, "An agent? An agent for who?" "For the United States Government," Marguerite responded. "I am just sure of it. While Lee was in Russia, I got many personal letters from him...but what was so strange, I had no idea where he was. Finally, I traveled to Washington, D. C., and went to the State Department. There, I was given the red carpet treatment and assured not to worry. Lee was fine and was living in Minsk, Russia, and had married a young Russian girl named Marina Nikolaevna Prusakova."

As the visit came to an end, Oltmans wrote, he had a sense that for Marguerite Oswald kindnesses and friendships were few and far between. It was etched in her face for all to see. With a big hug, the two parted ways, promising to stay in touch.

CHAPTER THREE

Upon returning to Hilverson, The Netherlands, Oltmans resumed his reporting job with NOS Television. Small stories and interviews were his assignments - no world-class reporting - but it was at least a job, and it gave him hope once again that his journalistic career wasn't over.

It was June of 1964 when NOS Television program director Carel Heinz Enkelaar. a long-time producer, informed Oltmans that he would be accompanying "the world wonder Gerard Croiset", the Netherlands' greatest clairvoyant, known throughout Europe as "The Amazing Dutchman", on a whirlwind tour of the United States. Oltmans was to be his translator.

Jack Harrison Pollack of Doubleday Publishing authored an astonishing biography of Gerard Croiset that first brought his amazing story to America and the world. Croiset often proclaimed, "I am Croiset The Great" and "Everyone has the same gifts as I have. With me, they are a bit more developed. Everyone is in contact with other people. I just feel these contacts a bit more intensely".

Gerard Croiset

"The Amazing Dutchman" was born in North Holland in 1909, where he lived a fairly conventional early life. According to Croiset, he became aware of his extraordinary gifts once he began working for a local watch maker. He began to experience visions and future events that pertained to the life of his employer. It was these early occurrences that set him on the path he would follow throughout his life.

Croiset's fame grew to the point that word of his abilities spread beyond the Netherlands. He continued to explore the potential of his gifts and began to conduct psychic healing as well. After becoming established. he opened a clinic that allowed members of the general public to come to him for healing and consultations.

During the course of the tour, which included both large cities and small towns across America, he and Oltmans became good friends. People overflowed the capacities of arenas and auditoriums at every stop. And they all seemed to come away amazed and astonished by the feats that Croiset performed.

Oltmans' personal notes tell of the incredible mind power that Croiset displayed and how he himself would be awestruck by the accuracy of his visions. Over and over, from one stop to the next, Croiset left people shocked and astonished by his mental abilities.

Well-known to police and private investigators throughout The Netherlands, Croiset had become a valuable asset in locating missing persons and helping to solve murder cases. Law enforcement agencies all over Europe and the United States and as far away as Japan had called upon him to utilize his unusual powers. As with most paragnosts, he did not solve every case. But many, many times, his visions proved to be correct and helpful.

After the tour ended, it would be February 2, 1967, when Oltmans would see Gerard Croiset again. They met in the office of Carel Enkelaar, and as the three talked, Croiset mentioned a very strong and clear vision he had experienced concerning the assassination of President Kennedy.

He explained that what he had seen was a man who was behind the actions of Lee Harvey Oswald - someone with whom the accused assassin had a very close friendship...even an intimate father-to-son relationship. This individual had a double name with the letters "O" and "SCH" in it. He had dealings with the oil world and was possibly a geologist.

The vision was one of his clearest ever, Croiset told them. He had seen multiple people shooting at Kennedy from opposite directions and had seen a white car that was positioned behind a wooden fence. And $900,000 dollars was paid for the deed. The mysterious man had "pushed" Lee Harvey Oswald to set in motion this huge, historical event for political purposes. He was, simply, the driving force behind the killing.

Willem Oltmans, Gerard Croiset and Carel Enkelaar

Oltmans and Enkelaar sat in silence in that small, crowded office, contemplating what they had just heard. Taking into account the accuracy of many of Croiset's previous visions, could this be what was needed to help resolve the many remaining doubts and questions surrounding the greatest crime of the century?

Finally, Carel Enkelaar spoke up and asked what they should do. It was agreed that they should keep details of the powerful vision private until Oltmans could make his next trip to the United States and arrange a meeting with Marguerite Oswald. He would then ask her if Lee ever had a friendship or relationship with an older man who fit Croiset's description.

On March 10,1967, Oltmans departed for a lecture engagement in Los Angeles, California, to be followed by a flight to Dallas to meet again with Lee Harvey Oswald's mother. But on the way to Texas, he began to develop a low fever and a noticeable swelling under his left arm. Upon arrival at the airport, he took a taxi to Parkland Hospital. During his examination, the physician – Dr. Ralph Greenlee – noticed Oltmans' deep European accent and asked where he was from and why he was in Dallas. Oltmans replied, "I am from Amsterdam, The Netherlands, and I came to interview Marguerite Oswald."

"Very interesting lady, that Mrs Oswald," Dr. Greenlee said. "I had a keen interest myself in the events that went on following the assassination of President Kennedy." He invited Oltmans to his home for a drink after his shift at the hospital was over. The two men had an enjoyable time together, talking until the wee hours of the morning.

The doctor revealed that he had not been present at the hospital on that fateful day but had since talked with many of his colleagues who were in attendance when the President was brought in. And every one of those other physicians had cast doubt on the official version of the details regarding his wounds. Many would not step forward out of fear.

As dawn approached, Dr. Greenlee drove Oltmans back to the Dallas Hilton Hotel in his red Ferrari.

On March 11, 1967, Oltmans arrived at Marguerite Oswald's home once again. She greeted him with a big hug and a cheerful smile. After some brief small talk, he posed the question in as subtle a manner as possible: Did Lee ever have any close friendship with an older person, leading up to the time of the assassination? He didn't mention Croiset's vision. Instantly, Marguerite replied that he most certainly did...and the man's name was George De Mohrenschildt. "Why do you ask such a question?" she inquired.

She went on to say that it was a very close friendship between the two and that it had always bothered her. This person was involved in something to do with the oil business in Dallas and was wealthy. "Why was this man around my son so much and what did he want from my Lee?" she wondered. "I never could understand this friendship. My son worked in a schoolbook warehouse and made $1.25 an hour, and this man was in the oil business and was even referred to as a Baron. I have many times wondered if this was a real friendship or was this man George De Mohrenschildt just out to use Lee in some form?"

It was very clear by the serious tone of her voice that Marguerite suspected something just was not right with this so-called "friendship". She very calmly stood up and walked to a large bookcase in her living room. There, in perfect numerical order, were the entire twenty-six volumes of the Warren Report. She took out Volume 9 and stated that it included the Commission's investigation of that mysterious individual.

"Doesn't it seem strange to you that there are 118 pages of testimony of George De Mohrenschildt? That's more than any other individual that the Warren Commission investigated. More pages than Lee's wife Marina, more than Jackie Kennedy, more than Jack Ruby, more than anyone else that the Commission called in concerning the assassination."

From a folder, Marguerite brought out a copy of a personal condolence letter - sent just twenty days after President Kennedy had been assassinated - from George de Mohrenschildt to Mrs. Janet Lee (Bouvier) Auchincloss, the mother of Jacqueline Kennedy:

Port-au-Prince, Haiti

Dec. 12, 1963

c/o American Embassy

Dear Janet:

May I ask you to express my deepest sympathy to your daughter and tell her that both my brother and I will always remember her as a charming little girl from East Hampton. So many sorrows have been ruining her young life.

Since we lived in Dallas permanently last year and before, we had the misfortune to have met Oswald and especially his wife Marina sometime last fall. Both my wife and I tried to help poor Marina who could not speak any English, was mistreated by her husband; she and the baby were malnourished (sic) and sickly. We took them to the hospital.

Some time last fall we heard that Oswald had beaten his wife cruelly, so we drove to their miserable place and forcibly took Marina and the child away from the character. Then he threatened me and my wife, but I did not take him seriously. Marina stayed with the family of a childless Russian refugees for a while, keeping her baby, but finally decided to return to her husband. Somehow then we lost interest in the Oswalds.

It is really a shame that such crimes occur in our times and in our country. But there is so much jealousy for success – and the late president was successful in so many domains – and there is so much desire for publicity on the part of all shady characters that assassinations are bound to occur. Better precautions should have been taken.

Remember our discussion one day on the plane from Dallas to Washington? We spoke of criminal children and of the terrible problem of delinquency in the South. Oswald is just an expression (of) that cancer which is eating American youth.

You will excuse this rambling letter but I was just sitting in my office thinking of the strange fate which made me know Jackie when she was a little girl – and which made me also know the assassin (or presumable assassin) his wife and child. And your daughter has been of such help to the Cystic Fibrosis Research Foundation – which we had started in Texas several years ago. She was an honorary chairman of the Foundation.

I hope that Marina and her children (I understand she has two now) will not suffer too badly throughout their lives and that the stigma will not inflect the innocent children. Somehow, I still have a lingering doubt notwithstanding all the evidence of Oswald's guilt.

I have just received a letter from my bother (Dimitri) and he also recalls of our friendship with you and extends his deepest sympathy to you and your daughter.

Please accept my feelings of respect and consideration.

Sincerely,

G. de Mohrenschildt

Further research into the friendship between George de Mohrenschildt and Janet Lee Auchincloss showed a serious intimate relationship that came close to resulting in marriage. The two met in the summer of 1931 and became romantically involved while spending time at the Auchincloss family estate at Hammersmith Farm in Newport, Rhode Island. It was on those grounds that the wedding of Jacqueline Bouvier to Senator John F. Kennedy took place. It's widely known that young Jacqueline was fond of George de Mohrenschildt and even referred to him as "Uncle George".

"I have always found this friendship between Lee and George de Mohrenschildt so very strange and unusual," Marguerite reiterated. "How did my son fit in with this man? And now a letter like this showing he knew Jackie Kennedy's mother. It's so very strange. I just have a very strong feeling he has, in some way, put my son in the position as he ended up, concerning the assassination of President Kennedy."

CHAPTER FOUR

Once again the two parted ways, and Oltmans recorded in his notes that he wondered if he had stumbled onto the key to the entire assassination mystery. He now knew that Gerard Croiset's vision of the man he had seen behind the plot to kill John Kennedy closely matched the description of de Mohrenschildt. The "O" and the "SCH" were in his name. He was involved in the oil business and a trained geologist. And he was older and had a close father-son type of relationship with Lee Oswald. It was all falling right into place.

There was but one thing left to do, and that was to locate and interview George de Mohrenschildt himself. Unable to find him while still in Dallas, Oltmans returned to New York City and contacted Carel Enkelaar with the news that Marguerite Oswald had named the man who had matched the details of Gerard Croiset's vision. Upon hearing this, Enkelaar instructed Oltmans to find him and set up an interview as quickly as possible.

Sensing a major worldwide story and an exclusive for NOS Television, Enkelaar told Oltmans also to do a full background check on George de Mohrenschildt. As both men discussed this strange friendship, Enkelaar began to ponder whether they were getting very close to the center of what could have been a major conspiracy.

November 22, 1963, began like any other day in Dallas, Texas. An early morning shower and a gentle breeze had freshened the air over the prairie land that surrounded the city. As coffee perked and the citizens awoke to clearing skies and a Fall sunrise, many knew that Dallas would be front and center in the daily news. President John F. Kennedy and the First

Lady would be there, along with Texas Governor John Connally, Vice-President Lyndon Johnson and their wives.

A motorcade was scheduled to travel from Love Field to the downtown area. Large crowds were expected. As the appointed hour drew close, people began to line the main roadways and streets, eventually standing eight to ten deep along the planned route. The first of the vehicles passed, generating a cheer that became a roar that grew to fill the cavernous spaces between the buildings. Excited onlookers jostled one another for a better view, often spilling off of the curb.

Then, finally, there it was. The huge blue Lincoln Continental glistened in the bright sun, its plexiglass top having been removed to allow a better view of the occupants. The President and First Lady were seated in the rear, and in front of them, John and Nelly Connally occupied two fold-down jump seats.

Senior Special Agent Roy Herman Kellerman rode in the passenger seat, and Special Agent William Robert (Bill) Greer was driving. Greer was a Secret Service veteran, having joined in 1945 and previously served as driver for Presidents Roosevelt, Truman and Eisenhower. Kellerman had been a Michigan State Police Trooper prior to joining the Secret Service in 1941.

The custom-built 1961 Lincoln Continental Presidential Limousine had been created by Hess and Eisenhart of Cincinnati, Ohio. The Ford Motor Company leased it to the United States Government for $500 a year. Kennedy himself had selected the stunning Navy Blue color, which had never before been used on any Presidential vehicle.

The coach was 21 feet long and weighed over 7,800 pounds. Its specially-fitted, see-through, non-bulletproof top was configured in six sections for easy removal and storage in the trunk, where space was made available by mounting the functional spare tire continental-style on a large rear bumper. The Secret Service code name for the limo was "SS100X".

The motorcade was to end at the Trade Mart, and a luncheon would be served. Then, the caravan would drive back to Love Field, where the dignitaries would board Air Force One for their return trip to Washington. As the line of cars and police motorcycles slowly crept through the streets of downtown Dallas, there was no reason to expect that all would not go as planned.

Suddenly, as the big Lincoln made a hard left turn onto Elm Street, a sharp sound echoed across Dealey Plaza. Many of those present took it to be just a motorcycle backfire or possibly a firecracker going off. But then a second, identical noise was heard, and people who had been standing along the roadway were ducking and diving to the ground. Children were being pushed down and covered by their parents.

The unthinkable had happened. Shots were being fired at the President. And one more was to come. To some, they were clearly three distinct rifle shots. But others claimed to have heard as many as six or seven. No one knew it at the time, but in the mere six to eight seconds that it took for those shots to be fired, the John F. Kennedy administration had been brought to an end.

It was Noon in Dallas. The President of the United States was being targeted for assassination. The first Secret Service Agent to take action was Clinton J. "Clint" Hill. Realizing something was terribly wrong, he leaped from the follow-up Secret Service vehicle (nicknamed "The Queen Mary") and dashed for the Presidential limousine. Climbing aboard just as Greer accelerated and fled Dealey Plaza, Hill scrambled over the trunk area and positioned himself protectively over the President and Mrs. Kennedy.

Inside of the car, he witnessed a bloodbath. Governor Connally was lying on his side in his wife's arms, having suffered multiple gunshot wounds. Collapsed on the First Lady's lap, the President was bleeding profusely from a massive head wound. Recalling that nightmare scenario years later, Clint Hill was still shaken by the horror of what he had seen up close. He mentioned giving a thumbs down sign to the Secret Service followup team, indicating that the very worst had happened.

What had started as a happy, sun-filled day was now enveloped by unspeakable sorrow. Years later, Nellie Connally would describe an eerie silence that filled the car after the shooting. No one had said a word, as the mortally-wounded John Kennedy was rushed to Parkland Hospital.

The onlookers remaining in Dealey Plaza were in total shock. A large number of them ran for the knoll that backed up to a railroad yard and a small parking area. Meanwhile, members of the Dallas Police Department found themselves overwhelmed with information and trying to gain control of the situation. Shortly after the shots were fired, their radios were reporting that an officer had been shot in the city's Oak Cliff section.

All-points bulletins were issued to be on the lookout for a white male, possibly in his early 30s, armed with a high-powered rifle. Within ninety minutes of the shooting, a suspect was already in custody. The greatest manhunt in the state's history was over almost before it had started. And America and the world would soon witness perhaps the lowest point in the history of Texas-style justice.

A 24-year-old former United States Marine, Lee Harvey Oswald, had been arrested. With one hour, his name and infamy would spread across the United States and reach the far corners of the world. Initial reports revealed that he was employed at the Texas School Book Depository as an order filler. The Depository faced Elm Street, where the limousine had been fired upon. Oswald appeared disheveled and not to know exactly why he had been apprehended. And he repeatedly and vehemently denied any involvement in whatever he was suspected of doing.

While being moved from one interrogation room to another, Oswald was paraded through the hallway, past a throng of news reporters. Tom Pettit of NBC shouted out, "Did you shoot the President?" In what sounded like a quivering voice, Oswald replied, "No, I didn't, I didn't shoot anyone. I would like some legal representation, and the police won't allow me to have it. I don't know what this whole situation is about, and I ask that someone please come forward and help me with legal representation."

Then, from the crowd of reporters, came another shout: "Did you kill the President?" And the reply: "No, they have taken me in because I have lived in the Soviet Union. I'm just a patsy." In Willem Oltmans' private notes, he wonders if that phrase "I'm just a patsy" has some kind of connection with George de Mohrenschildt. And his close examination of de Mohrenschildt's past produced some startling findings.

A picture emerged of a highly-polished intellectual who had worldwide connections at the very highest levels. He was born in Mozyri, Byelorussia, in 1911 - the son of Sergi Alexander Von Mohrenschildt, who held the title of "Marshall of Mobility of the Minsk Province" and was the region's representative of the landowners to the Tsar.

He was a descendant of Russian royalty and was said to be of Prussian, Polish, Swedish and Austrian royal blood and related to Prince DeMohrny, heir of Napoleon, and Tsar Nicholas. The Von Mohrenschildts were considered to be "White Russians", which was the term used to identify those who fought the communist "Red Army" during the civil war that followed the revolution of 1917.

Schooled in Poland, Belgium and the Netherlands, George de Mohrenschildt would go on to earn a PhD in International Commerce at the University of Liege, Belgium, in 1928. Records show that he spoke as many as ten foreign languages. In 1938, after arriving in America, George would change his name from Von Mohrenschildt to "de" Mohrenschildt. When asked why, years later, he replied that the Von was used by German families and he feared having to endure the pressures that might come with his having a German name.

During World War II, de Mohrenschildt had ties to both French and German Intelligence. One startling revelation in Oltmans' notes was his connection to Adolph Hitler's Chief of Intelligence, General Reinhard Gehlen.

By the end of World War II, Gehlen had brought his vast underground network of Nazi spies to work for America's Central Intelligence Agency (CIA) as the Gehlen Organization. And that group is where we find a link between the two men. In 1941, de Mohrenschildt had worked closely with his cousin, Baron Constantine Maydell, in New York City. Their business used the name "Film Facts", and it was known to have produced several pro-Nazi documentaries.

Records also revealed that Baron Maydell was one of North America's top Abwehr agents - recruited personally by General Gehlen in the post-World

War II era. The Abwehr group was a Nazi Intelligence-gathering organization. In the mid 1950s, the Gehlen organization trained and schooled its spies at the CIA's clandestine military base at Atsugi, Japan. That's where Lee Harvey Oswald was stationed and trained in the U2 Spy Plane program.

General Reinhard Gehlen

On June 2,1941, de Mohrenschildt was detained by two Special Agents assigned to the Attorney General's Office in Corpus Christi, Texas. Eugene Wilson and Russell Brown reported that he had been observed sketching and taking photographs of the Coast Guard Station and ship channel at Port Aransas. The agents reported their suspicions that de Mohrenschildt was a German spy.

Government documents also reveal that as early as October of 1942 the U.S. Department of State had placed a red flag on de Mohrenschildt's passport file because an investigation had shown that he was thought to be a Nazi agent. Such a move dictated that special attention would be paid to whether he posed a security threat to the United States.

CHAPTER FIVE

I t was March of 1967, and Carel Enkelaar more than ever realized that what they had learned from their close look into the background of the man whom Gerard Croiset had seen in his vision and Marguerite Oswald had named just didn't add up. His bizarre friendship with Oswald had all the earmarks of some type of intelligence operative at work.

At the end of that month, Oltmans was finally able to contact de Mohrenschildt by phone. Upon hearing that NOS Television of Hilversum, The Netherlands, was interested in doing a personal, filmed interview, he readily agreed to a meeting. But soon, even more disturbing information regarding his early years came to light.

Oltmans' investigation showed that de Mohrenschildt's first job in the United States in 1941 was employment with Pierre Fraiss, the Chief Export Agent for the Shoemaker Company of New York. And records revealed that Fraiss was connected with the French Intelligence organization. Working as a salesman, de Mohrenschildt traveled throughout the United States gathering information on people who were involved in pro-German activities. The evidence was clear. George de Mohrenschildt had been spying for the French, as well.

As the layers of his life are peeled back, a picture emerges of a man of intrigue and mystery. He had many dealings in the oil business worldwide and with the United States State Department, which was very guarded regarding his exact involvement. Records revealed a very unusual three-thousand-mile walking trip that George and his fourth wife Jeanne undertook. It wound through Mexico and Central America, only to end at the Cuban exile training camps in Guatemala City - on the eve of the CIA-backed invasion of the Bay of Pigs.

In another unusual find, records show that in November of 1959, the de Mohrenschildts, while on a business trip to Mexico City, were invited to a personal meeting with Anastas Mikoyan, who was at the time the second most powerful figure in the Soviet Union under First Premier Nikita Khrushchev.

In Oltmans' personal notes, he reported that Jeanne de Mohrenschildt had boasted that she had invited Mikoyan to come to Dallas, where she would prepare a real American-style dinner for him. Even more documents would surface showing that the Office of Naval Intelligence, the FBI, the CIA, the U. S. Customs Agency and the Immigration and Naturalization Service all had extensive files on George de Mohrenschildt. The CIA's file was classified as "SECRET".

How could this person with so many strange connections and a past littered with international intrigue become the closest friend of the accused assassin of President Kennedy? Once Carel Enkelaar heard Oltmans' findings, he was sure the investigative journalist had uncovered someone who quite possibly had a direct connection to the Kennedy assassination. He felt that it was now becoming evident that there had indeed been a conspiracy - and it would be NOS Television that would break the story to the world.

Realizing that Oltmans could possibly be in danger, Karl Lenklloyd, the head of National Dutch Television, instructed him to inform the U. S. Justice Department that NOS Television was beginning an investigation into President Kennedy's assassination and would be starting with a taped interview of George de Mohrenschildt to discuss his possible involvement.

The morning of April 3, 1967, a direct call was made to Tim Hogan, Press Secretary for Senator Robert F. Kennedy, notifying him that NOS Television would be conducting a full investigation and would need recommendations as to what steps should be taken for their safety. The press secretary instructed Oltmans to come at once to Senator Kennedy's office on 43rd Street in New York City. The Senator was away in Albany but would be returning in the afternoon.

Later that day, Hogan called back to say that Robert Kennedy refused to speak of his brother's murder and would pass NOS Television's security concerns on to the FBI. In fact, the Senator had called J. Edgar Hoover personally, and Hoover had turned the matter over to the Criminal Division. Oltmans was told to await contact from the agency.

And so he returned to his apartment in Kew Gardens, Long Island. Then, much to his surprise, he received a direct personal call from Robert Kennedy. He wanted to know why NOS Television was conducting an investigation of George de Mohrenschildt. Oltmans explained that information had been obtained showing that de Mohrenschildt had been closely involved with Lee Harvey Oswald prior to the assassination.

Senator Kennedy warned Oltmans in no uncertain terms to stay away from the de Mohrenschildts, saying that both George and Jeanne were very dangerous people and both should be avoided. He urged Oltmans not to interview or become involved with them, expressing concern for his safety. Oltmans' notes document that conversation and Kennedy's remarks. Several hours later, two FBI Agents named Adherre and Jauss showed up at his door. Oltmans described the meeting in detail and how he felt like he was being cross-examined.

They asked question after question regarding why he was interested in George de Mohrenschildt and what type of information had been collected on him. Per his instructions from NOS Television, Oltmans repeatedly told them that he was just a journalist on assignment. But the interrogation went on for over two hours. When the agents left, he had been led to believe that his activities would be monitored and he would receive protection from the Federal Bureau of Investigation.

The next evening, Oltmans was driving his Sunbeam Tiger sports car along 23rd Street in Manhattan. He suddenly had a feeling that a dark sedan was following him. When he changed lanes, it stayed so close that he felt it might hit his vehicle in the rear. Becoming concerned, he decided to take the 53rd Street exit. As Oltmans accelerated and moved to the exit lane, the dark sedan increased its speed dramatically and moved forward as if to pass him. At the last second, however, the driver cut Oltmans off and forced him almost head-on into a guard rail.

The tremendous impact destroyed the Sunbeam, and Oltmans struggled to remove himself from the crushed car. Dazed and confused and bleeding from the forehead, he saw the sedan exit and disappear into traffic. After being treated at a hospital, he returned to his apartment and noted in his diary that he was certain that the car following him had purposely caused him to crash.

In detail, he described that the sedan had many chances to pass but stayed glued to the rear of his sports car until he made his move toward the exit. It was the first car wreck of his life, and it happened within just 24 hours of his contact with the FBI. He felt strongly that the incident was no coincidence.

After several days of remaining close to home, Oltmans made plans to return to The Netherlands. He was now apprehensive that other "accidents" might follow. When he was told about the crash, Carel Enkelaar ordered the Dutchman to return to Hilversum. He spent the entire summer at his parents' bungalow at Huis ter Heide, recuperating and planning his next step.

In October of 1967, Oltmans returned to New York and once again initiated contact with George de Mohrenschildt. Still a bit fearful after his last encounter with danger, he had resolved to move in a much more guarded fashion. Finally reaching de Mohrenschildt by phone, he set up the first interview.

NOS Television had made an arrangement with the Dallas CBS affiliate station to assist in the filming. It would take place in the de Mohrenschildt's apartment and last for about forty minutes. During his early morning flight, Oltmans recalled, he had felt nervous and somewhat uneasy at the prospect of being one of the very few who would enter the strange and mysterious world of George and Jeanne de Mohrenschildt. But as he had been forced to do so many times before in other circumstances, he would rise to the occasion.

CHAPTER SIX

A rriving at the appointed time, Oltmans was greeted by a tall, robust, dark-tanned, middle-aged man dressed in tennis shorts and a light-colored polo shirt. In a strong Russian-Polish accent, he said, "Welcome. I'm George de Mohrenschildt." The gentleman had wavy, grayish hair and eyes that were light blue and crystal-clear.

Oltmans recorded his initial impression of de Mohrenschildt as someone who was smooth, confident and suave. And then Jeanne de Mohrenschildt joined them. She had strikingly sharp features and dark, piercing eyes, and she was wearing a long, flowing solid black dress. Her first words were, "Welcome to our home."

George and Jeanne de Mohrenschildt

It was obvious to Oltmans right away that these were not your average next-door neighbors. The apartment was rather small and sparsely-furnished but cozy and comfortable. Tennis balls and several rackets lay in a corner. The stale smell of cigarette smoke hung in the air. As they sat down to talk, Oltmans asked George why he had given permission now to be interviewed when in the past he had refused all such requests. In his notes, he wrote that de Mohrenschildt stared straight into his eyes and responded, "I give this interview only to ease my conscience."

With the tape rolling, George began by mentioning that he spoke ten different languages and Jeanne spoke five. He went on to describe his early years, recounting his family's escape from Russia to Poland and the hardships they had faced during the war years. He talked of being on the brink of starvation and almost freezing to death. It was like hearing tales taken from a history book, and the room was totally silent as he spoke. But Oltmans noticed that many details were glossed over; de Mohrenschildt's words were carefully chosen, and his tone was somewhat guarded.

When the subject turned to the death of his only son Sergei from cystic fibrosis, his eyes filled with tears and his voice became more hushed, as if he could barely speak of the tragedy. The sorrow that filled his heart was evident to everyone in the room. In a somewhat awkward exchange, he mentioned that Jeanne was his fourth wife, and she responded sharply that this marriage would not be his last, either.

Oltmans asked about their friendship with Lee and Marina Oswald, and George expressed his anger regarding the treatment they had received from media outlets in the United States and around the world. He had been so relentlessly badgered that he began to turn away any and all who searched for him and his wife seeking information concerning their relationship with the Oswalds.

In Argentina, a publication had shown a doctored picture of him running alongside President Kennedy's car in Dallas and wrote that he was involved in the murder and had killed the President himself. Another bizarre story had him in Dealey Plaza on November 22, 1963, standing on the curb on Elm Street dressed in a black flowing cape. He supposedly pulled out an automatic handgun, fired multiple shots at the limousine, hitting both John Kennedy and John Connally, and then covered the weapon with his cape and slowly walked away, escaping detection.

Did de Mohrenschildt think Oswald killed Kennedy? He replied, "Absolutely not," citing a time well before the assassination when Lee expressed how much he respected the young President. (In a side note,

Oltmans wondered how he felt about John Connally, the man who had denied an upgrade of his military discharge when he was Secretary of the Navy.)

When asked if he were in fact a "rich oil man", as reported, de Mohrenschildt admitted that was a fair description but bemoaned the fact that media constantly used that term when mentioning him. No question appeared to fluster his interview subject, so Oltmans pressed on. Had big oil money been behind the assassination? "That's pure bullshit," was the quick response.

The conversation turned to the Jim Garrison investigation in New Orleans. George said he thought Garrison was on the right track but doubted that he would succeed. This case could be solved but not without a full understanding of the Cuban refugees and their complicated situation. When asked about the Warren Commission, he became very agitated and defensive, saying that the whole thing was nothing but dirty laundry and vicious rumors.

Instead of bringing a group of detectives in to solve this case, de Mohrenschildt observed, they formed a group who did nothing but collect information. And very little of what they collected even had anything to do with the assassination. The Commission, he continued, did everything possible to put forth an acceptable conclusion that Lee Harvey Oswald had committed the crime and had done so by himself. Both George and Jeanne expressed dismay at how the Commission had twisted their testimony around to a point at which, when the final report was released to the public, they didn't even recognize their own words.

Suddenly, Jeanne stood and pointed her finger at her husband. "Mischka," she said, "let them hear the truth." In the Russian language, "Mischka" means "the bear". It was the name she called George in private. The couple told Otlmans that they had given Marina Oswald a box of record albums that would assist her in learning to speak English. With a look of disgust, Jeanne said that Marina was lazy and showed no interest. She didn't care if she could speak the language or not.

It was in the spring of 1963. and the de Mohrenschildts were preparing for their move to Haiti. They gave no further thought to the albums. But when they returned to Dallas in 1966, they found that the Oswalds had returned the box. Inside was a picture of Lee holding a rifle with a telescopic sight and wearing a holstered revolver. On the back was written "To my friend George from Lee Harvey Oswald". The date on the photo was April 5, 1963. It was the exact same image published by Life magazine after the assassination – the one many people at the time believed to have been doctored.

The interview threatened to go off track on occasion. Jeanne's voice rose angrily as she said they would file a lawsuit against the Warren Commission if they could do so without violating their privacy. At one point, Oltmans was asked how his grandmother spelled her middle name. Sometimes it was hard to tell if George was joking, but in those instances every attempt was made to steer the discussion back to the serious subject at hand – the Kennedy assassination.

Asked if had he ever met or known Jack Ruby, de Mohrenschildt snapped, "Absolutely no!" He went on to say that he found Ruby to be a very hideous individual. He told of a letter that Ruby had sent to a local Dallas newspaper saying "I have something to tell. The murder of President Kennedy went differently than people think." Instead of appearing on the front page, it was hidden deep inside as if it were not that important.

As the conversation turned once again to the Garrison investigation, Oltmans asked George if he would consider being interviewed by the DA. He expressed a small fear of a meeting with Garrison because "in fact, he is on the right track." He was investigating groups whose members hated Kennedy, and the Cuban refugees were prepared to kill the President. "To understand these Cubans, George said, "you must first realize they live by a different code of honor. Cubans who are involved in murder would rather shoot themselves than to betray someone." As Oltmans continued with that line of questioning, George showed great interest in the fact that Garrison had named the CIA as having involvement in the assassination.

It was at that point that George told Oltmans that he could not continue. Standing and moving to the center of the room, Jeanne said, "Mischka, we must be behind Garrison. If there is a God, we must try to help Garrison." Not wanting to let the interview end, Oltmans pressed de Mohrenschildt once again on his overall view of the Warren Commission. But each time that subject was brought up, George appeared to become completely disgusted. He explained that he was annoyed by the silly questions and their personal nature. At one point, he asked impatiently, "How in the name of God does the price I paid for my horse when I was in the Polish Cavalry have anything to do with the assassination of President Kennedy?"

In the end, Oltmans had filled up a lot of pages and collected plenty of facts - but he felt that the nearly two hours had essentially been a waste of time. However, in his private notes he said he sensed that he had earned de Mohrenschildt's trust and confidence. No American journalist had succeeded in being granted such access.

Oltmans' notes give full credit to the vision by clairvoyant Gerard Croiset. Without that, he admitted, he would never have begun his search for the truth behind the Kennedy assassination. He and de Mohrenschildt had bonded over family stories and their years of study, and Oltmans felt that a friendship had developed. George recognized the Poslavsy name as nobility and added that the heritage was Polish. As the two men parted, they spoke of planning for a subsequent visit.

CHAPTER SEVEN

Oltmans' next step was a trip to the office of New Orleans District Attorney Jim Garrison. It was February 11,1968, and their investigation was in full swing. The place buzzed with activity: people rushing about, phones ringing and typewriters clacking. At the rear of the cavernous space was the command center, from which America and the world first heard the names of those whom Garrison had uncovered and become convinced were part of the assassination plot.

Oltmans described "Big Jim" Garrison as a giant of a man, leaning back in his chair with his feet up on his desk. There was a holstered pistol strapped to his side. He was surrounded by awards, plaques, wartime pictures and family photos. File cabinets and overflowing bookcases lined the walls, and Oltmans commented on the presence of works by Plato and Aristotle.

Jim Garrison

This, clearly, was the epicenter of the action. In his no-nonsense way of speaking, Garrison volunteered right away that "they" would have to murder him to shut his mouth and curtail his efforts. "Nothing can stop me from keeping this examination going until the truth is reached," he said. "This whole investigation started by pure accident. Once this office learned Lee Oswald had spent the summer of 1963 in New Orleans, we felt compelled to take a look into his actions from that summer and who he was associated with here in our jurisdiction. And we found plenty.

One individual who became known to us in our investigation was David William Ferrie, a New Orleans resident who had been seen with Lee Oswald that summer of 1963."

A main target of the Garrison investigation, Ferrie was well known to have been involved with an anti-Castro group who had actively trained in jungle guerrilla warfare for a possible attack on the Cuban nation.

James Phelan, a reporter for the <u>Saturday Evening Post,</u> perhaps described him best: "You had to see David Ferrie to believe him. And once you saw him, you never forgot him."

He was 48 years old and completely hairless due to a medical condition called *alopecia praecox.* A bizarre and clown-like figure, Ferrie wore glued-on eyebrows and had tufts of hair fastened to random places on his head with spirit gum. He had a nasally voice, an aversion to soap and a penchant for making authoritative statements.

Ferrie had been a teacher, an unsuccessful candidate for the priesthood, a pilot who was discharged by Eastern Airlines for homosexual activity, a psychologist with a degree from a diploma mill, a private investigator, a self-proclaimed cancer cure researcher and a amateur hypnotist. Despite all this, in later years many who knew David Ferrie personally described him as brilliant.

David Ferrie

Garrison continued, "We had witnesses that connected Ferrie and Oswald together during those summer months of 1963. We had found some strong evidence that Ferrie had connections with the CIA as a pilot. Our office located one witness who placed Ferrie in Texas on the day of President Kennedy's assassination. We found a lot of unusual things that had transpired leading up to November 22, 1963. Once we learned more of Ferrie's background, we were sure we were on the right trail and indeed our investigation revealed there had been a plot hatched and planned in February of 1963 in New Orleans to kill John Kennedy."

Oltmans could tell that Garrison was carefully choosing each and every word he spoke concerning his case. As the meeting came to a close, he took the opportunity to mention George de Mohrenschildt. Garrison replied that his office was very interested in contacting him and that his mysterious background warranted a much closer look. He even went as far as to say de Mohrenschildt greatly fascinated him and that the Oswald/de Mohrenschildt friendship proved that there was much more to this case and it was much bigger and broader than the Warren Commission had reported to the American people.

The Garrison narrative opened a Pandora's box. The characters involved might easily have sprung from a lurid mystery novel. There was the seamy underbelly of New Orleans exposed for all to see, seething with pure hatred and evil intent to assassinate the President of the United States. The whole case was one huge cesspool that turned the stomachs of most Americans. In the end, Garrison did bring charges against a prominent New Orleans businessman named Clay Shaw.

During a lengthy trial, he tried to prove that Shaw had worked as an agent for the CIA. But as to whether the defendant had been involved in a conspiracy to assassinate President John F. Kennedy, a New Orleans jury found him not guilty of the charge. When polled, the members stated their belief that, while they couldn't convict Shaw, there was sufficient evidence to indicate that there had been a conspiracy.

Years later, in his testimony before a congressional committee, former head of the CIA Richard Helms did confirm that Clay Shaw had indeed been a contact agent for the organization and was at one time on the payroll. He had been granted covert security approval in December of 1962 and was involved in Project QKENCHANT. Other familiar names connected to that CIA project were E. Howard Hunt and G. Gordon Liddy.

As the Shaw trial ground to a close, Oltmans realized that he needed to separate himself from the New Orleans debacle and set his sights once again on strengthening his relationship with George de Mohrenschildt. The Dutchman had already gone further than he had dared to believe he could. His driving force now was to break the biggest news story of his life. The world was about to see Willem Oltmans at his finest.

His Garrison interview had been filmed by NOS Television, and it aired around the world on February 21, 1968 – creating a surprising amount of interest in the ongoing drama in New Orleans. In Oltmans' private notes, he expressed shock that certain media groups had chosen to broadcast his work, considering that none had used any of his investigative stories since the New Guinea affair. In fact, NOS Television was given credit but no mention was made of Willem Oltmans by name. It was hurtful and wrong, and once again he felt the pain of having being rejected.

That feeling had dogged him for many years, and there seemed to be no end in sight. Frustrated and feeling helpless, he handled the rejection as he had since it all started: by digging in once again and continuing to report. This was his life and his profession, and no one was going to stop him.

Oltmans arranged to return to New York. He added to his notes Jim Garrison's comment that Vice President Lyndon Johnson most likely had prior knowledge of the plot to kill John Kennedy. It was quite a reach for him to make such a statement or even to contemplate the possibility. Would the American people ever believe that something so cynical, dark and evil could occur in the United States? Garrison went on to say, "Just take a look at who Johnson appointed to investigate the assassination. All hand-picked, all had close ties to the CIA."

Allen Dulles had been fired as the head of the CIA by President Kennedy. He was chosen to serve on the Warren Commission, Similarly, Senator Richard Russell had been the powerful chairman of the Senate Arms Services Committee, which wielded great control over the CIA. Gerald Ford, a member of Congress, was well-known for his connections with the CIA through the House of Representatives. And John McCloy had been the head of the The Office of Strategic Services (OSS), the World War II predecessor organization of the CIA. Now this unusual group of public servants was chosen to determine the truth behind the President's murder. "Something doesn't seem right with this picture," Garrison had said.

Oltmans himself had wondered why certain news media outlets in the United States had been so quick to accept the Warren Commission's findings and then employ the power of television to try to convince Americans that there had been just one man and three bullets that had ended Kennedy's life. Leading the charge had been CBS News anchor Walter Cronkite, who used his evening broadcast to try to convince an already skeptical public that the Commission's report told the true story. Oltmans' notes from that period reflect a clear disrespect for what the country had come to regard as news reporting.

Chapter Eight

In May of 1968, Willem Oltmans spoke with his manager, Robert Keedick, concerning his New York lectures. During that conversation, he mentioned his car crash and how he had the strong feeling that it was intentional. Somewhat concerned, Keedick recommended that Oltmans set up a meeting with Robin Moore, an American writer. The two men arranged to get together that very evening at a small quiet, out-of- the-way bar on Third Avenue in Manhattan.

After a cordial greeting, Moore introduced Oltmans to an associate by the name of Glenn Smith. With his close-cropped hair and dark sunglasses, Oltmans noted, he looked very much like the popular image of a secret agent. Smith presented a business card showing he was an attorney-at-law with Florida address. And both he and Smith, it turned out, were engaged in an ongoing investigation of the assassination. This short meeting struck Oltmans as somewhat strange and unusual, with Smith fishing for any information he might have uncovered. At the end, they all agreed to get together again in the future and compare notes.

In late summer of that year, Oltmans received a letter from Glenn Smith requesting that they meet in Utrecht, The Netherlands. The Hotel Terminus was chosen as the site, and Carel Enkelaar would also be in attendance. This meeting also turned out to be of a suspicious nature, with Smith asking to see every bit of data they had collected.

Suddenly, he jumped to his feet and, within inches of Oltmans' face, issued a warning: "It's time for you to stop your investigation, Willem." With a cold, calculated stare, he added, "You wouldn't want to be picked up on the streets of New York and hustled into a car and then driven to a private airport and flown miles out over the Atlantic Ocean and then pushed out, would you? You would not be the first one to die prematurely being involved in the Kennedy case."

Picking up his already packed bag, Glenn Smith - without saying another word - turned and walked out the door. Sitting stunned and speechless, Oltmans realized he had just been threatened. Furthermore, his efforts later that day to find information on Smith were fruitless. There was no attorney by that name in Florida, and the address on his card was fictitious.

Taking into account the car crash and then this face-to-face direct threat, Oltmans and Enkelaar knew they had aroused a sleeping giant. They were getting too close to the core of something huge, and their efforts were making some people very uncomfortable. After a long discussion, the two decided that for safety reasons the investigation would pull back and let the dust settle. They would wait out the remainder of the summer before taking their next step. And that would prove to be a trip to Los Angeles on August 28, 1968.

Loran Eugene "Skip" Hall

During the summer months, a confidential lead had pointed the investigation in the direction of a thirty-nine-year-old soldier of fortune by the name of Loran Eugene "Skip" Hall. A hard-nosed, no-nonsense soldier ready at a moment's notice to go and fight communism anywhere in the world, Hall considered himself a conservative but not a fascist. He spoke openly of being a member of an elite fighting group who smuggled weapons from Florida into Cuba and had landed on the beaches of that island with the intent to murder Fidel Castro.

Hall had steely, piercing eyes and an oversize dagger tattoo on his arm. He bragged that he relished a good fight and, even more, loved to see blood flow.

Records revealed that he had been connected with Interpen (International Penetration Force). He also had ties to the IACB (International Anti-

Communist Brigade), where a fellow member had been David W. Ferrie. one of the key objects of the Garrison investigation.

NOS Television had arranged for a local CBS affiliate station to film the interview. As the cameras rolled, Loran Hall made a stunning admission. It shocked all who were present. In a stern, straightforward manner, he declared that on October 17,1963, just 36 days before the murder of President Kennedy, a man named Lester L. Logue was offered $50,000 to join a conspiracy to carry out the assassination.

Not wanting to name the individual who offered the money, Hall did go on to say that the person was a well-known petroleum engineer. He further mentioned that there were five people present in the room that day. Oltmans' notes reveal that when pressured to supply the names of those others who witnessed the offer, Hall would provide only a description of one. He said the man was the owner of a large national trucking company. But he stated that he would supply the names one-by-one if Lester Logue refused to corroborate his statements.

It should be mentioned at this point that Oltmans, realizing that this story could potentially become explosive on a worldwide scale, made sure to capture every word on tape and to ask questions two or three times to gather every word and nuance. He expressed in his notes how grateful he was that members of the camera crews from CBS were also hearing this powerful and incriminating disclosure. As Oltmans methodically conducted his questioning of Hall, he began to realize the momentous importance of what he had uncovered and the impact that what this soldier of fortune had told him could have on history.

When the interview came to an end, Hall called Oltmans to the side and asked to be paid $500.00 for the information he had just given. "There's no way NOS Television will pay you that much money," Oltmans told him. "A small token for your honesty, possibly, but we don't pay for stories. We just find them and report them. Our policy at NOS Television and the way we work is to give the accused parties the chance on film to confirm or deny the statements that have been lodged against them."

Looking around the room, Skip Hall then repeated his promise: "I am telling the absolute truth, and if Lester Logue denies that this is what happened that day, I will name each one by one of the five persons present in that room the day the offer was made."

The film in its entirety was rushed by mail back to NOS Television in Utrecht, where a decision would be made regarding when to air it for the public to see. Meanwhile, Oltmans left Los Angeles by American Airlines on another trip to Dallas, where he would be met at the airport by George and Jeanne de Mohrenschildt. He was to be their house guest. He was greeted at the airport with big hugs from both. It was obvious by then that he had succeeded in earning their trust and respect.

As George and Jeanne's grey Ford Pinto wound through the downtown streets, a light rain began to fall. Darkness was approaching, and the damp pavement mirrored headlight beams coming from all directions. As they turned onto Elm Street, an old red brick building loomed on the corner – the infamous Texas School Book Depository, standing alone among the shadows of its past. An eerie silence filled the car. "Ever been in Dealey Plaza?" George asked. Turning to face the back seat, he said, "What a pity that assassination was."

The three continued the drive toward the de Mohrenschildts' apartment. Oltmans wrote of telling George about his meeting with Loran E. Hall. He went on to say that Hall had mentioned a man named Lester Logue. "Have you ever heard of this man named Logue?" he asked. George responded, "Yes, I know him very well. We've been very close friends for many years. We did oil exploration studies together in Cuba when Cuba was run by Fulgencio Batista. We're both members of The Dallas Petroleum Club."

As the car pulled into the apartment parking lot, Oltmans told the de Mohrenschildts that Hall had been in a meeting with five individuals in addition to Lester Logue. He explained that this Loran Hall was a soldier of fortune fighting against communism and mentioned that on October 17, 1963, a well-known petroleum engineer from Dallas had offered Logue $50,000 to participate in an assassination plot against President Kennedy. At that point, George hurried to get Oltmans settled, obviously anxious to hear more of his old friend Logue.

"We have it all on tape and it's on its way to the Netherlands as we speak," Oltmans told him. "NOS Television will make a decision on when to release it to the public." The journalist's notes go into great detail about George's reactions to hearing this startling disclosure by Skip Hall. His usually quite serious demeanor had faded, and he appeared to be quite amused by learning of the thorny situation in which his old friend Lester Logue now found himself.

Asked if Logue had yet been informed of these accusations lodged against him, Oltmans replied that he had not. But he intended to call him to ask for a filmed interview. Smiling with amusement at the cat-and-mouse game he was playing, de Mohrenschildt suggested that Oltmans call him from the apartment phone. "But," he admonished, "don't dare tell him you're here in my home and let's see what he says."

The call was made, and once Logue was informed of what had been said concerning him, he exploded in a rage of cursing and yelling. The entire time, George listened with one ear tipped close to the receiver as if to hear every word said. Smiling and slapping his knee several times, he appeared to get great enjoyment and pleasure out of hearing Logue wiggle and squirm as he denied it all and said he indeed knew Loran Hall and he was nothing but a pill head psychopath.

Then, losing his composure completely, Logue threatened to file charges against Oltmans and have him arrested. He said he would call the FBI and say this was all fabricated...and Oltmans' only goal was to garner publicity. But when the offer was made for him to tell his side of the story in the interest of fairness, Logue agreed to sit for a taped interview the next day.

CHAPTER NINE

Willem helped George and Jeanne to prepare for a small dinner party planned for the evening. The guests would be Max and Gali Clark. She was a former Russian Princess, a member of the three highest orders of Russian nobility and well known throughout Dallas. Max Clark was an attorney and had formerly been the head of security for General Dynamics Corporation.

As the evening progressed and the drinks kept flowing, it became obvious that Jeanne had consumed more than her limit. Her words were slurred, and she once again adopted a noticeably sarcastic tone when addressing George. That made the small gathering feel uncomfortable, Oltmans' notes reveal.

As the conversation moved from local events to more personal subjects, de Mohrenschildt mentioned the letter he had sent to Miss Janet Auchincloss, Jacqueline Kennedy's mother, after the murder of Robert F. Kennedy. In her response, she said that in her heart she would always think of John F. Kennedy as a hero. George's rather strange reaction was, "Well, if the Kennedy family aren't interested in solving the murder of John Kennedy, who would be?"

Oltmans would record in his notes that as his friendship with George grew, it became obvious that he harbored strong and bitter resentment toward John Kennedy and the entire Kennedy family.

After the evening drew to a close and the guests had left, Oltmans wrote of just George and himself finally sitting together, sipping vodka and telling stories of their past. Feeling restless and still not ready to end the day, de Mohrenschildt recommended that the two take a walk. It would be the first of many private, intimate moments the men would come to share.

The apartment complex that the de Mohrenschildts lived in was occupied by individuals with a variety of sexual orientations - from swingers to bisexuals to homosexuals to transsexuals. It was, according to Oltmans' notes, a very lively environment. The grounds included a paved walkway along a narrow and heavily tree-lined area that ran past the tennis courts. This, hidden behind the cover of thick foliage, was well known throughout the area as a meeting place for sexual activities.

Over the next decade, Oltmans would visit and stay as a house guest from two to three times each year. And he and George would take many walks down the path. Both men were very private regarding their personal relationship. On many occasions Jeanne accused George of being a homosexual and resented the closeness that he and Willem had developed. At one point, she even insisted that she be allowed to go along on their walks together. But they always moved quickly, leaving her far behind and angry.

Records would also reveal that one of George's four wives, Dorthy Pierson, had openly accused him of having abnormal sexual preferences and claiming that he would sodomize his partners. That marriage lasted but eight months. Another ex-wife, Wynne Shaples, made the same charges – along with infidelity. In their divorce proceedings, George mounted a defense - until Sharples threatened to expose him in open court. He then quickly withdrew his challenge and accepted the divorce decree.

On October 22, 1968, the Loran Hall interview was aired by NOS Television in The Netherlands. It generated very little interest, and the story they expected to be a worldwide sensation seemed never to make it across the Atlantic. Oltmans was on a lecture tour in Los Angeles at the time of the broadcast. He had been allowed no input, which disappointed him, as he was sure he had brought a long-held secret to light. His personal notes show him wondering whether this was just one more attempt to discredit him and his journalistic work. Would it ever end?

Bitter and disillusioned, Oltmans stubbornly refused to stop and give in to whatever force was working against him. He resolved that if Americans hadn't heard the story when it aired in The Netherlands, then Willem Oltmans would bring it back home and make it public. On April 1,1977, he appeared on the ABC television show "Good Morning America", with David Hartman. To a stunned host and audience, Oltmans told of the $50,000 being offered to Lester Logue to take part in a plot to assassinate President John F. Kennedy, as exposed by Loran Eugene Hall in Los Angeles on August 28, 1968.

It was almost ten years after the story first broke in The Netherlands, and American news media were finally clambering to get access to it. Lester Logue issued a full denial and threatened both Willem Oltmans and ABC News with a lawsuit. None was ever filed. Newsrooms around America pushed for some kind of proof concerning the Hall allegations. Things were heating up, and the narrative that once seemed doomed to oblivion took on a new life nationwide. Oltmans requested that Carel Enkelaar release the entire raw film of the Loran Hall interview, saying that NOS Television had nothing to hide.

Staying at the de Mohrenschildts' apartment as George's guest proved at times to be quite challenging. The bickering and arguing between him and Jeanne was almost a daily event. The two fought and cursed each other over even the simplest things. Witnessing them at each other's throats day after day, Oltmans would note that he was happy to be single. "How do you stand this?" he would ask George. "What would I do without her?" was the reply. It was a love-hate relationship off of which they both seemed to feed.

With more and more of these visits, George and Willem had created a unique friendship based upon mutual trust and caring. And this bond enabled George to express some of his most guarded thoughts and feelings.

One striking example revealed in Oltmans' notes was his statement that Americans are in general brainwashed to accept what their government leads them to believe.

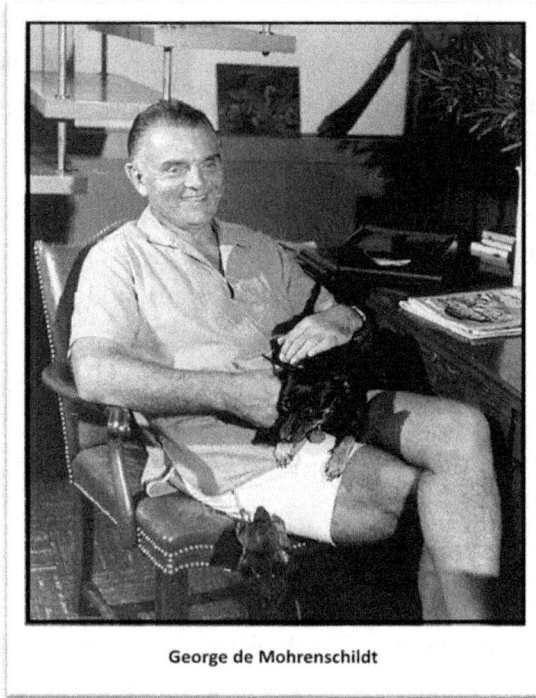

George de Mohrenschildt

For example, de Mohrenschildt said, a large amount of false and exaggerated information has been fed to the average citizen promoting the threat of Communist aggression. And it has gone on for so long that the people now believe that lie. "Communism is not the enemy," he continued. "Johnson, Humphrey, and Nixon are the real enemies. The American establishment is the enemy.

I absolutely have no hope for America. I could not care less if this country were blown up by a hydrogen bomb."

CHAPTER TEN

As his lecture tour continued, Oltmans made stops in small-town America and brought his first-hand account of world events to small gatherings such as civic groups, which consisted mainly of women middle-aged and older. Describing his typical audience to George, he said they tended to be senior citizens, with some getting around with walkers or wheelchairs. But at times they did ask good questions. And George responded, revealingly, "I must confess I would rather go to bed with another man than go to bed with one of those old fossils."

It was January of 1969, and Oltmans had traveled from Chicago to Dallas. Arriving by cab at the de Mohrenschildt apartment, he found that George was gone. And Jeanne wanted to talk. She began what would become an almost non-stop monologue. It included great detail regarding her husband's first three marriages.

With a somewhat sinister smile, she revealed that she herself had been married four times. And George's daughter Nadya from his third marriage had come to stay with her father after having being expelled from school in Pennsylvania for using LSD. She was extremely ill and required an oxygen tent at night and almost constant care. Oltmans described her as having black, rotten teeth, Coke-bottle-thick glasses and flowing blond hair.

As evening approached, George returned home. A gathering with friends from the neighborhood had been planned, and soon the small apartment was filled with laughter and conversation. At one point, George talked of the difficulty of providing for Nadya. That prompted this response from her: "You can bet one God damn thing. I sure as hell didn't ask to be born."

At that point, everyone fell silent. Her head low and her feelings crushed, Nadya left the gathering. Oltmans mentioned in his notes that her comment stuck with him for days. The hopelessness of her situation was heartbreaking. What kind of father could hurt his daughter that way? He found the event to have been a waste of his time and the guests quite boring, and he was glad when it all ended.

The following day, which was the 25th of January, Oltmans made a call from the de Mohrenschildt apartment to Marguerite Oswald. George stood by, listening intently. Marguerite was quite agitated and could not believe that Oltmans was at the couple's home. When he explained that the de Mohrenschildts were preparing a book and would be interested in meeting with her, she instantly replied that she would never agree to that under any circumstances and that she wanted nothing to do with those people.

Later, before they were to depart for the Dallas Petroleum Club, the two men took one of their long walks together. George asked for Willem's assistance in turning his manuscript into some publishable form. Agreeing to help prepare it for submission to a publisher, Oltmans suggested that NOS Television create a complete film to use as a companion piece for the book.

That evening, as Oltmans' notes detail, he had a private talk with Nadya. He could see that the situation with her terminal illness left her bitter and hopeless, feeling that she had no one to turn to for help. "She was one of the saddest young persons I had ever met," he wrote. Unable to offer any guidance or advice, Oltmans was heartbroken. He held Nadya in his arms with tears in his eyes and told her, "You are loved."

At times, it seemed as though their two dogs were the thread that held George and Jeanne together. Nero and Cinderella were chihuahuas – small in size but huge in personality. Both of the de Mohrenschildts were pet lovers and talked to their dogs like they were their human children. And it was nothing for Jeanne to sleep with Nero and Cinderella and carry them wherever she went.

The morning of January 26, Oltmans was enjoying a cup of coffee and getting ready for his return to New York. Cinderella suddenly jumped onto his lap and licked him right on the lips. Seeing him wipe away the canine kiss, Jeanne jumped to her feet, furiously proclaiming that her dogs were cleaner than most people. She reached down and picked up Nero, cuddled him and said, "You can kiss Momma."

Nadya commented, "Jeanne, I've seen you kiss those dogs right on their asses before." Even more angry and responding in a very loud voice, Jeanne said, "You shut your mouth!" Then she grabbed Cinderella and kissed the dog on the vagina and scooped up Nero and kissed him right on the his penis. As Oltmans stared in disbelief, she declared, "So now that proves that dogs are cleaner than people. What in heaven is more clean than a dog? I would never dream of kissing George there or any other man."

This incident was among many involving the dogs that he recorded in his notes. Apparently, there was at least one during each of his visits. He referred to Nero as "the crown prince of the family" who ruled the roost. On another occasion, Jeanne told of a trip she and George took to Jamaica. The dogs had been quarantined at the airport. When she learned that they were to be held for twenty-four hours, she threw a fit and made a spectacle of herself by staying with them in the impound. She slept in their small cages and came out only when the dogs were brought out to walk or defecate.

Leaving Dallas aboard American Airlines for a lecture engagement in New York, Oltmans pondered his next move involving the de Mohrenschildts.

He contacted NOS Television and reported to Carel Enkelaar that the friendship had been formed and strengthened and that he would be returning to Dallas in February to film another personal interview.

In his notes, he describes his slow, methodical approach to illuminating the bond between Lee Harvey Oswald and George. By ever so slowly chipping away, he was letting de Mohrenschildt reveal in his own way and at his own pace what the real relationship was between the two men. An appointment was set for a filming at the Dallas CBS studio on February 14, 1969. During that interview, George would give his impressions of Lee Harvey Oswald as he knew him in 1962.

The very first meeting between Lee Oswald and George de Mohrenschildt took place at 2703 Mercedes Street in Fort Worth. It was a city with its share of fine homes, manicured lawns and stately drives, but the Oswalds had rented a wood-framed duplex from Chester Allen Riggs, Jr. The dwelling was small but livable, and it came furnished with just the basics.

The area was known for its high rate of rental turnover and was mainly filled with transients, day workers and people down on their luck. Hard work and hard times were commonplace for those who called Mercedes Street home. The Oswalds would live there from July of 1962 through October 1962. With $59.50 a month rent and a $12.00 utility bill, they got by on Lee's small weekly paycheck from the Leslie Welding Company.

During the early summer months of 1962, George had learned from White Russians living in Dallas of a young couple who had just returned from the Soviet Union. Eager to find out more, he spoke to George Bouhe, one of the community's organizers. It was then that he heard the story of an American and former United States Marine named Lee Harvey Oswald, who had defected and tried to renounce his American citizenship, only to reconsider and ask to return to the United States after just two years with his new Russian-born bride and baby daughter.

It was a tale right out of an international suspense novel, and it intrigued de Mohrenschildt, as it later did many others. Bouhe went on to say that some in the White Russian community had bad feelings regarding the Oswalds. They did provide some help but felt that, though they couldn't put a finger on it, something just wasn't right with this strange pair. For one thing, the speed and the ease with which they had been allowed to leave the Soviet Union didn't ring true.

One member of the local Russian group had said that only after a wait of several years had he received permission from the authorities to emigrate – and after he had relocated in the United States, it had taken three years for the Russian Government to notify him that a family member had died. Their suspicions aroused, a large portion of the community resolved not to invite the Oswalds to any more group gatherings.

Some went so far as to speculate that Marina was some sort of agent slipped into America on a secret mission. Others simply felt that Lee was a strange individual who somehow would bring trouble to their peaceful lives. Far from being inconspicuous, the Oswalds were constantly surrounded by an aura of mystery and intrigue that tended to create an uneasy feeling in most who met the young couple.

In July of 1962, de Mohrenschildt met the Oswalds for the first time. He visited their home, accompanied by Colonel Lawrence Orlov, a personal friend and business associate from Fort Worth. As the two men approached the rundown rental house, they got the clear impression that the two were living in poverty. George knocked lightly on the door, and it was opened by Marina Oswald. Speaking in Russian, he told her that the local Russian community wanted to offer friendship and would like to know how they could help.

Oddly, he identified himself to her as George Bouhe. (Oltmans noted that George gave no explanation for using the false name.) Twenty-one-year old Marina invited the visitors to sit and enjoy some sherry. After a few minutes of conversation, a door opened and Lee Harvey Oswald entered the room. Rising to greet him, George repeated his reason for them being there.

Lee, then twenty-two and a small-framed man, appeared to be curious but had an air of caution about him. Eventually, speaking in fluent Russian, he accepts their offer of friendship. Almost immediately, de Mohrenschildt said, he felt that the bond of a friendship was forming. "I must hear of your days in Russia," he told Oswald. Finally, Lee would have someone he could talk with and could trust.

Lee and Marina Oswald

The very next day, the Oswalds traveled by Continental Trailways bus from Fort Worth to Dallas for dinner with the de Mohrenschildts. Listening intently to every word Lee said, George would come away impressed by the young man. His idealism and dreams made him seem wise well beyond his years.

Speaking of his days in Russia, he said that never once had anyone tried to convert him into becoming a communist. There were no attempts at intimidation or brainwashing.

CHAPTER ELEVEN

O swald spoke of America with bitterness. He called the far right-wing groups fascists. It was his belief that the American system worked for the wealthy, leaving the lower class to struggle in low-paying jobs and with few educational opportunities. In his view, America's political leaders were substandard. George found Lee to be very articulate and well-read. The two shared many of the same ideals and beliefs. They talked until late in the evening.

Meanwhile, Marina had taken Jeanne aside and was telling her in private that Lee was abusive and violent at times. Feeling frightened and intimidated, she found herself wondering how much longer the marriage could last. She revealed that their sex life was dull and almost non-existent. In the kitchen of the de Mohrenschildt home, the young wife could finally tell someone of the pain and sorrow that engulfed her life due to her broken marriage.

Marina Oswald

Oltmans was leaving Dallas for New York in February, 1969. During the drive to the airport, George began to open up and offer some of his thoughts about Lee Harvey Oswald. He believed that it was very possible that Lee had, as was reported at the time, taken a shot at General Edwin Walker. Lee despised the man, he recalled, and all that he stood for. "It's just a thought," he said, "but no one will ever know for sure."

George went on to say, "I'm confident Lee did not shoot President Kennedy. When I trained young boys in the Polish Army who were cold, steel-eyed sharpshooters, it took a certain type of individual, and Lee did not have this in him. He was nervous, young and uncoordinated, and most of all didn't have that killer steel look in his eyes."

"Knowing Lee as I did, had he killed the President, he would have proudly admitted it and offered a reason. That was his way. He saw himself as a revolutionary and boldly would have taken credit for the act. Instead, he denied doing it over and over and finally shouted to the newsmen, 'I'm just a patsy!' In those twenty hours of interrogation, he would have spelled out just why he had killed Kennedy and for this cause.

"He told the absolute truth and was completely innocent. I believe the Dallas Police knew it. He was not the picture that has been painted of him. He was an intelligent, articulate young fellow who had a different view on many things that most Americans believe in. But he was not a killer and did not assassinate President Kennedy. It's a shame; the poor man's soul should be freed from this injustice. Since the assassination, many have said that I mentored Lee Oswald, which to a degree is true. But Lee had formed many of his beliefs way before he had ever met me. He had rejected American society even as a youth."

In Oltmans' private notes, he highlights two startling statements that George made on February 16, 1969: "You know, Lee was very set on me and would do anything I told him to do. He was very easily led along. Had I asked him to shoot Kennedy, he would have done it without question." and "How would you react if one day it did come out that I had organized the assassination of President Kennedy?"

As the car neared the airport, the two men sat in silence. What George had just said was earth-shaking to the journalist. He noticed that his friend was staring straight forward, motionless and showing no emotion. Was that a confession? Had George de Mohrenschildt just implicated himself as the organizer of the plot that killed President John F. Kennedy?

Later, on the flight back to New York, Oltmans thought back to that February day in 1967 when Gerard Croiset, in the office of Carel Enkelaar, had told of his clear vision of an assassination plot. The pieces had fallen right into place: the mysterious individual with two last names and an "O" and "SCH" in the last one...the trained geologist who worked in the oil business...the older man who had a father/son relationship with Lee Harvey Oswald.

A reading of Oltmans' notes made during this period reveals his innermost thoughts regarding his close relationship with George de Mohrenschildt. It's evident that he conducted himself in the manner of a professional journalist while dealing with his subject and did not apply any undue pressure.

And so, on each of those occasions when de Mohrenschildt revealed more details of his involvement with Lee Oswald leading up to President Kennedy's assassination, his revelations were made in his own words and given to Willem of his own volition. Those admissions were made over the span of a ten-year long investigation and friendship.

In June of 1969, Oltmans was receiving letters from George on the letterhead of "The Dallas Petroleum Club". In one such correspondence, he complained of his treatment while he was teaching at the University of Texas and doubted that he would return, saying that he had become too controversial. Even though the students seemed to like him and many had asked him to stay on, some of the faculty members - mainly right-wingers - had even spit on him. "They're all nothing but a bunch of disguised Nazis," George wrote. "I'm sure I will look elsewhere to teach."

In July, even more letters arrived - this time on "The Camden Oil Company" letterhead. "What an amazing incident with Senator Edward Kennedy and that young girl Mary Jo Kopechne on Chappaquiddick Island," George wrote. "It will surely point the finger once again at the strange, ruthless Kennedy family. I assume this will be the end of the ongoing adultery of those Kennedys. It's more than time that the good name of Lee Harvey Oswald is purified."

Oltmans' notes reveal how openly de Mohrenschildt now expressed arrogance and resentment and contempt regarding the Kennedy family - unlike in George and Jeanne's Warren Commission testimony, where they praised them. In a surprising twist, George asked Willem to correspond from that point on via his business address, to keep their conversations private from Jeanne.

In September of 1969, George wrote that he had been offered a professorship at primarily black Bishop College in Dallas. He felt that it should work out well, and he would no longer have the long drive to Austin. Most important of all, he wouldn't have to face those far-right Nazis who taught there. His next letter arrived in November of 1969 and asked Oltmans to spend Christmas in Dallas at their apartment, saying that things couldn't be better, their health was excellent, they were in great mental condition and the new teaching position at Bishop College suited him well.

In closing, George wrote of the news that Police Chief Jesse Curry was going to be retiring. He had announced he now felt free to tell the truth about Oswald. "Imagine this scoundrel now after all these years of keeping his mouth shut fearing he would lose his job will now say Oswald was indeed innocent, de Mohrenschildt mused. "It's so typical."

CHAPTER TWELVE

A letter on the Camden Petroleum Company letterhead arrived in September of 1970. Things were going well at Bishop College and George would try to set up a speaking engagement for Oltmans. "The students are wonderful," he wrote. "Even the hard activist ones are nice. It was a very special letter you sent to Nadya. She greatly appreciated it and admitted she had a real weak spot for you. Everything here in Dallas is still the same. One big dung hole, things never change. Come and see us soon. We miss you."

In a subsequent letter that Oltmans received on May 5, 1970, de Mohrenschildt commented that President Lyndon Johnson now believed there was a good possibility that more individuals were involved in the Dallas murder. "It was reported by Walter Cronkite, that skunk," George fumed. "If you think how LBJ and that skunk Cronkite nailed Lee Oswald to the cross, it's just plain sickening."

He went on to say, "We had a strange occurrence at a local party several weeks ago. We ran into Marina Oswald. She refused to speak to us in Russian. She's a one hundred per cent American housewife now. It was easy to see she knows where the butter on her bread comes from. She told us she had not contacted us because she feared we were mad at her. I've always thought someone should look into her and her background much more closely. She treated Lee with such hatred and such meanness."

Over the course of the next several months, Oltmans traveled the lecture circuit in America with stops in small towns and big cities alike. With his charismatic style and dashing looks, he continued to charm small groups all across the country. His next letter from de Mohrenschildt, on July 16, 1970, seemed a little strange and different. George wrote, "I am just back from Pakistan. I first went through Rome. It was all so rushed. Our stupid government never gives you enough time to do for yourself."

In Oltmans' notes, he recorded that the letter never explained why he went to Pakistan - only that he had been sent by the United States Government. He commented that "all the way to 1970, George de Mohrenschildt was doing tasks for the US Government." Later, through sources he did not reveal, Oltmans would learn that George had been sent by the the International Cooperation Administration (ICA) to Yugoslavia.

Fall classes at Bishop College had begun, and de Mohrenschildt mentioned that in the opening ceremonies all of the professors would be wearing black robes. "Oh, well," he observed, "it's better wearing those than a Nazi SS uniform."

Nearly nine months later, on May 1, 1971, George wrote "You must come to Bishop College for a lecture, the students will love you. We are playing tennis, and all in the house is going good finally. We miss you, come for a visit. I am greatly jealous of your upcoming trip to Moscow. Wish I was going along. You will finally breathe real fresh air. A trip to Europe does not interest me. It's way too tame there. Europe reminds me of a 45-year-old woman, degenerate with no appeal but maybe with some possibility to interest you. It never seems to amaze me how Americans are just like a group of charming monkeys. One has so much fun with them. The only oasis of peace and tranquility is in our apartment."

And then, about a month later, Otlmans received another correspondence – this one sent as registered mail, which was an option George had never before chosen. In it, de Mohrenschildt implored, "Please promise me you will never under any circumstances give the recorded tapes we made together to any government agency. These tapes are for us to sell and make as much as possible - maybe even a figure like $10,000. If something were to happen to me, please see to it that my fifty percent share goes to my daughter Alexandra. Come and stay with us, we miss you."

In September of 1972, Jeanne met Oltmans upon his arrival at the Dallas airport, looking tanned and healthy. She reported that their beloved female dog Cinderella had died. During a very somber and quiet ride back to the de Mohrenschildt apartment, she told of her special love for her two dogs and that Cinderella had even accompanied her on the witness stand when she testified before the Warren Commission in Washington D.C.

With a very cold, devilish look in her dark piercing eyes, Jeanne recounted with great pride how Cinderella had snarled and showed her teeth to Attorney Albert Jenner, counsel to the Commission. Pulling back in his chair, Jenner said, "That dog won't bite, will it?"

A small dinner party had been planned for that evening, and the guest list was rather strange and unusual, to say the least. One couple was a very young, blond-haired fellow and his half-Chinese wife. A short woman who was said to be the best pistol shooter in all of Texas came with her husband, a black man dressed as a woman. He was a drag queen who performed at one of the nightclubs in downtown Dallas. And several homosexual friends of the de Mohrenschildts who lived in the apartment complex were there.

As the evening drew to a close and all of them had left, George and Willem headed to the swimming pool. In the darkness, the two men swam in silence. As during Oltmans' other visits, they had found their private moment together. On this occasion, he asked George if he thought the identity of the actual Kennedy killer would remain a secret forever.

George replied rather quickly, "I certainly believe one day someone will confess. The Cubans participated in the assassination because Kennedy had betrayed them at the Bay of Pigs invasion. And they were totally right in this. All the Cubans I know and knew at the University of Texas thought the same way."

As the men lounged in the pool late into the night, de Mohrenschildt recounted an incident in one of his classes at Bishop College. A very large black athlete who had often flirted with George did so one day right in front of the whole class. Finally George stopped the young fellow and said, "I actually love women." And the student replied, "Well, I *am* a woman."

George quipped that he had seen Julie Nixon on a morning television show, and if he had to marry a woman who looked like that he would become a homosexual overnight. Then he spoke of his good friend Tito X, who owned a large ranch on the US-Mexican border and was dying of drug abuse. He said people there in Texas lived like rats. No wonder some drank themselves into oblivion. Life in and around Dallas was a complete circus.

Oltmans had arranged for George to get together the following day with Dr. Cyril Wecht, a forensic pathologist who was known for his criticism of the Warren Commission's findings concerning the assassination of President Kennedy. Their talk was to take place at the de Mohrenschildts' apartment.

Dr. Cyril Wecht

George, rushing back from a meeting in downtown Dallas, encountered Dr. Wecht in the parking lot of the apartment complex. Greeting him, de Mohrenschildt said, "You found me." Oltmans reported that, from the very first moments of the visit, Jeanne was defensive, asking Dr. Wecht what his intentions were and why he was interested in George.

Replying diplomatically, Dr. Wecht said, "I only want to orientate myself better about Lee Harvey Oswald." The men talked in depth about the Bay of Pigs invasion, and George at one point compared the anti-Castro Cubans' hatred for John Kennedy to that of the Jews for Adolf Hitler

.

CHAPTER THIRTEEN

Jeanne repeatedly interrupted the conversation. Finally, Oltmans implored her to be quiet and let Dr. Wecht talk. She reacted angrily, shouting, "I am nothing but a dog! I am treated no better than a dog!" Disgusted by her behavior, the group gave up and ended their meeting, and Dr. Wecht departed. Jeanne continued her diatribe, telling George that he liked anyone who licked his ass. Saying nothing in response, George and Willem left the apartment to take a walk.

Upon their return, they were met at the door by Jeanne, who was very angry. She demanded to know what had been happening and where they had gone. Yelling at the top of her lungs, she raged, "I know very well where you've been. You've been on that path next to the tennis courts again. I had forbidden you, George, to ever go there again, and now you've gone there again!".

Now furious, Jeanne began to scream in Russian, as George and Willem stood there in silence. Oltmans, having had quite enough of her temper, finally left. When he returned, everything was quiet and back to normal. A leg of lamb had been cooked, and the rest of the evening was enjoyable.

Later, George would drive Willem back to the airport. In the privacy of the car, he commented that Oltmans was a good diplomat. He knew just when to leave and just when to return. "What can I do?" he asked rhetorically. "If I up and leave her, she'll drink herself right into a mental institution. I refuse to do that to her."

Oltmans then asked George how he should proceed regarding the Kennedy murder. Calmly, he answered, "Concentrate your investigation on the Cuban community in Dallas." Never before had de Mohrenschildt been so specific as to place the blame of the assassination of President Kennedy on the Cubans.

"It's plain to see the Kennedy family does not want to know what really happened in Dallas," George said. "The Kennedys are scared it will come out that in fact he died as a fool. Even the American people, it seems, don't really want to know what happened in Dallas - because they fear if the real truth is told, there will be a huge explosion and backlash." As always, George walked Willem right to the departure gate, and with big hugs the two parted ways once again.

On the flight back to New York, Oltmans recorded in his notes that he felt George was getting closer and closer to revealing more concerning the assassination in Dallas. In a way, he felt sorry for de Mohrenschildt. How could he stand living with Jeanne's madness and alcohol-fueled fits of rage? The constant bickering and badgering, her open jealousy and domineering ways? There surely would come a breaking point.

On one occasion, Oltmans remembered, he had mentioned to George that possibly he could come with him on a trip back to Russia, because he had many contacts there and they could travel together. But, like a coiled snake, Jeanne had snapped instantly that he would not be going to Russia and that all Willem was trying to do was take George from her.

The relationship between George and Jeanne was volatile. They fought each other not only with hurtful words but at times with fists. Their bickering at times was so intense that windows had to be closed. Neighbors stood outside and listened in disbelief as household items were thrown and screams and cursing could be heard coming from the apartment.

It's worth repeating at this point that Willem Oltmans recorded every aspect of his existence in his notes, meticulously detailed. At times, when he didn't have his notepad handy, he would write on napkins or even the skin of his hand for later transfer to a permanent medium. From momentous world events to the minutiae of his daily existence, he never relied upon his possibly faulty memory.

This went on for decades, and by the time of his death there were fifteen hundred ring binders of such diaries. And it's from the careful study of these notations that the authors have pieced together this fascinating tale of The Dutchman and The Baron. They're a record not only of Oltmans' work as an investigative journalist work but also of his private side.

For example, one can see that after a divorce in 1960, Oltmans' personal life moved in a different direction. While still remaining respectful of others' confidentiality, he became more and more comfortable with his own sexual orientation and less inclined to hide it.

In Dallas, Willem had told George of his fondness and even love for an aspiring young model by the name of Peter Van de Wouw. The relationship between Oltmans and Van de Wouw would prove to be a long one, lasting the remainder of his life. But, in his notes, Oltmans would reveal not from bitterness but in sadness that the two had shared a sexual experience just one time. Within the thousands of pages comprising the Oltmans diaries, the authors found many posed nude photos of Peter Van de Wouw. For the vast majority of their time together, the relationship would be of a platonic nature. But Oltmans referred to Van de Wouw as the love of his life, and he never went a single day without either calling the young man or writing a letter or sending a telegram. His entire personal life revolved around Peter Van de Wouw. George suggested that Willem bring him to Dallas and they could all fly to Mexico, where he had many friends.

Peter Van de Wouw

On one of his flights from New York to Dallas, Oltmans wrote in his notes that de Mohrenschildt had mentioned the attempted assassination of George Wallace, the Governor of Alabama. He felt it was a good thing, as Wallace could have ended up being very dangerous to the American society. In another even more chilling recollection, he recorded that right after George had made that statement, Jeanne - with a very dark and cold, sullen look - had said, "Seems there's no one prepared to shoot Nixon."

Quickly, George had replied, "That's the remarkable difference between a soldier who will shoot and kill for a cause or an idea and a killer who is hired and paid. The anti-Castro Cubans were prepared and murdered John Kennedy in Dallas without ever asking one penny for it."

In August of 1974, Oltmans wrote of receiving several disturbing phone calls from an unidentified individual warning of possible imminent danger to George de Mohrenschildt. Alarmed and worried, he called George in Dallas to relay the information and express his fears. In a very calm and steady voice, George told Oltmans, "To be honest, I don't much care now if I live long or not, although I would like to know who wants to do me in or have me disappear."

He revealed that he was thinking of accepting a payoff to leave the United States and move to live somewhere else. But he never said from where or from whom the offer had come. He added, "In case of my disappearance in murder or otherwise, you will be able to sell our filmed recordings. And remember that I want my daughter Alexandra to receive my fifty percent share."

Shortly thereafter, the breaking point was finally reached, and George moved out of the apartment he shared with Jeanne. He relocated to small, student-type housing on the Bishop College campus. No longer able to stand the haranguing and berating, he fled with nothing but his clothes. He felt it might be only a temporary arrangement, as the two could possibly work out their differences.

CHAPTER FOURTEEN

A few months later, on November 2, 1974, Oltmans flew from San Francisco to Dallas and was met by George and Jeanne. They were together again, trying to live in harmony. During the drive from the airport, de Mohrenschildt joked, "See, Willem? I still live. No one has got me yet." There were plans for dinner that evening with Pat Russell, the couple's attorney, at the Cipango Club.

For the first time in the seven years since their friendship developed, George asked that they not speak of the murder in Dallas. He wanted to wait until Russell was present. Oltmans recorded in his notes his curiosity regarding who might have offered this advice. The lawyer, perhaps?

Shortly after their arrival at the apartment, the two men left for a private walk - leaving Jeanne once again suspicious and on edge. They took their usual path. Willem once again brought up the possibility of George going to Russia. "You could do well there," he insisted. "With my contacts through the 'Club of Rome' and your fluent knowledge of the language, it could be a perfect fit." He offered the suggestion that George could be a go-between for business deals, and the idea did appeal to his friend.

Upon their return, de Mohrenschildt mentioned Willem's offer to Jeanne. That, as the two might have guessed, was a mistake. She exploded in anger and a blast of cursing. He would never go back to Moscow, Jeanne shouted. She went on a rampage around the small apartment, accusing Willem of once again trying to take George away from her. The blowup was one of her worst ever.

Disgusted anew by his wife's outburst of rage and jealousy, George walked out - leaving Willem to take the brunt of Jeanne's verbal assault. By then, she was shouting over and over again, "This will not happen! This will not happen!" When her husband returned, the crisis escalated. By this time, Jeanne had consumed too many vodka and tonics and was totally out of control.

Hurling insult after insult at George, she screamed out that he had told Nadya that if she felt she had had enough of this life she should just kill herself. "You shut your mouth!" George countered. To Willem, he said, "See? She's so drunk she doesn't know what she says." And the argument went on. In a bitter sarcastic tone, Jeanne accused George of beating her in the face and head after returning from a trip to California. "You were drunk once again," George said. "I had to stop you. You were out-of-control drunk." Finally, their tempers cooled – but everyone was left feeling miserable and disgusted.

The dinner with Pat Russell proved to be interesting but somewhat strange. The club catered to the rich and famous, from gangsters to the oil-wealthy. It was the epitome of first-class living in Dallas. Reportedly, one had to have a net worth of at least $100,000 even to be considered for membership – a not insignificant sum in the late 1960s and early 1970s.

In truth, most members were millionaires. $100 tips were commonplace. No matter what you were looking for, it could be arranged. Located on Turtle Creek Boulevard, the Cipango Club had a rich history dating back to 1946. The name referred to a mythical island sought by explorer Marco Polo - a place of untold wealth and pagan splendor. As described by Polo, "The people are dependent on no one, and their gold is abundant beyond measure."

Russell made his entrance in grand, flamboyant style, in a shiny new black Cadillac Coupe de Ville and sporting a three-piece, pin-striped suit and wingtip shoes. He had a young male companion at his side and loudly introduced him as Greg, his lover. This brash, open display of his homosexuality generated stares and hushed comments in the staid, white linen ambiance of the club's dining room. From the moment of his arrival, Pat Russell was clearly running the show.

Before even placing his meal order, he wanted to hear everything that Oltmans knew about de Mohrenschildt and the Kennedy assassination. George and Jeanne could only look on silently as the two engaged in their discussion. Beginning with Gerard Croiset's vision of a plot and the one individual who orchestrated the murder and set everything in motion, Oltmans recounted every detail that pointed the finger of blame at a person who happened to fit George's description.

Visibly nervous, with his eyes darting from side to side, George was tight-lipped but focused intently on everything that was said. He never once put forth a word of denial. Finally, Oltmans stopped. The crowded, darkly-lit Cipango Club bristled with energy. The white-uniformed wait staff hurried to clear tables. But the de Mohrenschildt table sat in total silence. Finally, speaking sharply in Russian, Jeanne said something that no one but George could understand.

Momentarily taken aback, Russell rubbed his chin and looked somewhat bewildered. Then he directly addressed George, saying "Never again talk to anyone about the assassination in Dallas without having me present." Turning to Oltmans, he admonished sternly, "Don't you create a story where there is no story." And with that, the meeting was over. Russell quickly stood and motioned to his young friend, saying, "Lets get out of here." Oltmans' notes indicate that George seemed more at ease once Pat Russell was gone.

Only moments later, de Mohrenschildt began describing an evening when four strange Latin men had arrived at their apartment, claiming to be from Life magazine. The couple knew right away that was untrue but let them in anyway. George said it was a very strange and somewhat tense encounter. One of the visitors produced an array of pictures showing several Cuban men and asked if they knew any of them. Looking closely,

George said that they did not. Jeanne joked seductively, "I don't know these men, but this one I would surely like to get to know much better." Her comment relieved some of the tension in the room.

Later, after the men were gone, she insisted that her light flirting was what had saved their lives. "Those men were out to kill us," she said. "It was a very frightening moment." From that day on, she said, they were afraid to answer their door. Oltmans' notes indicated that now, more than ever, he believed that George was somehow involved in the assassination plot, whether directly or indirectly. The stories he had told over the years, when pieced together, indicated a connection to the events that unfolded in Dealey Plaza.

As evening approached, George wanted to take a walk. The men headed down their regular path. But this time would prove to be different. Jeanne jumped to her feet and charged out the door with her dog in tow. "Wait for me! I'm coming, too!" she shouted. George and Willem maintained their regular pace as Jeanne continued to shout at them to slow down.

Finally, almost running, she caught up and went into another one of her tirades. "I'm treated like a dog!" she bellowed. "I am no Mexican woman. I will not walk behind you two. Let me get in the lead and you both walk from the rear." And those words enraged Willem enough that he finally confronted Jeanne. "You will never tell me how to walk or how fast to walk or where to walk," he told her. "I am through with you and your constant madness. Your jealousy and hateful ways have ruined you." Responding bitterly, she said, "What kind of thoughts have you gotten from George this time?"

"I will leave right now and never come back," Willem said. And with those words, he turned and walked straight to the apartment and began packing his bags. Feeling embarrassed and confused, George agreed to take Oltmans to the airport. The men agreed that their friendship would not end. They resolved that in the future they would meet privately without Jeanne present and correspond exclusively through the Dallas Petroleum Club.

As they said their goodbyes, George gave Willem a picture of himself surrounded by his students in his French class at Bishop College. On the back was written "To Willem, from the biggest crook in the Western Hemisphere". With a sheepish look, he said, "Now you can blackmail me with this picture."

Before boarding his American Airlines flight, Oltmans made a phone call to Marguerite Oswald. In a sad – almost pathetic - voice, she told him that she would no longer speak with journalists without being paid. Citing her expenses and the fact that little to no money was coming in for support, she said she now had no choice but to ask for compensation for her story.

This was to be Oltmans' last contact with her, other than an occasional letter that sent what she referred to as "flash sheets" - material she had gathered over the years concerning the assassination.

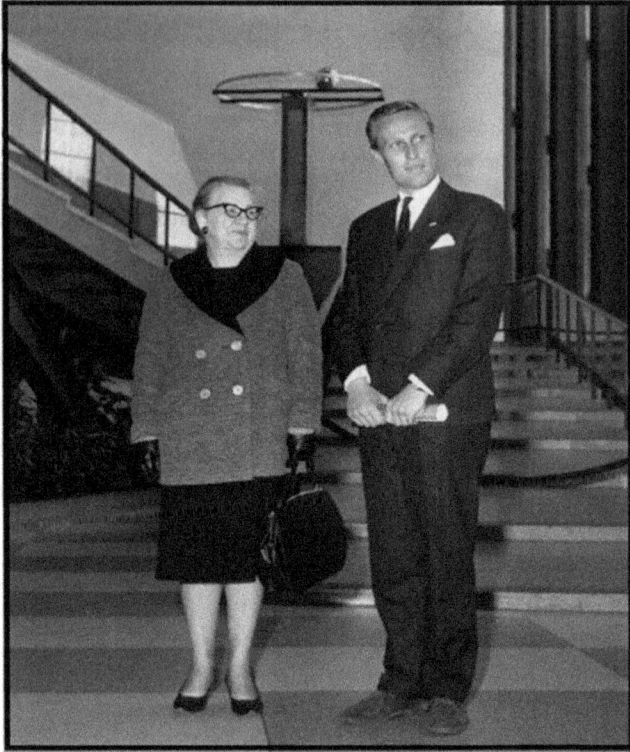

Marguerite Oswald and Willem Oltmans

As the years passed, she would become one of the most misunderstood individuals among those who had a connection to the events on that fateful day in Dallas. In the research for this book, the authors were able to locate one of her former personal friends: Steven Martin, formally from Hominy, Oklahoma. It was from him that we gained perspective regarding the "real" Marguerite Oswald.

He told us that she had been misunderstood from start to finish and got a raw deal from the national media at almost every turn. Only months after the assassination, his own mother, Shirley Martin, launched a personal investigation at her own expense into the facts surrounding the assassination. It would turn out to be one of the first real serious inquiries regarding what had transpired and the individuals who might have been involved. It was her early work, in fact, that spearheaded the drive to look beyond the findings of the Warren Commission.

With her family in tow, Shirley Martin would travel from Hominy to Dallas. One of her first contacts was Marguerite Oswald, and over time the two developed a personal friendship that lasted for many years.

Shirley Martin

Steven Martin remembers Lee Oswald's mother as being a lonely, tortured soul engaged in a desperate search for the truth. Until her death, she maintained her belief that her son was innocent. She insisted over the years that he was some type of agent for the United States Government and was set up to take the full blame for President Kennedy's assassination.

In the course of her long fight to clear the family name, Marguerite Oswald was belittled, shunned and ridiculed and viewed as being little more than a sideshow. She endured firestorms of anger and bitterness for the rest of her life – solely for being the mother of a presumed assassin.

Norwegian playwright Henrik Ibsen wrote "The strongest is the one who stands alone." Those closest to Marguerite Oswald described her as a brave and bold woman who never wavered or collapsed, despite the hatred that came her way. The Martin family referred to her as "Momma O".

Steven Martin spoke of their love and respect for her and allowed us to use his memories only if we would reveal the "real" person she was and not the caricature of her created by the outside world. He told us of falling ill with a fever on a visit to her home and how she had stepped in and insisted that he lie on her bed while she applied a cool washcloth to his forehead.

He fondly recalled that, "She fed me soda crackers and Seven-Up and showed the warmest love and compassion." It was this kind and gentle side of her that his family cherished – one that the world would never see.

CHAPTER FIFTEEN

On June 24,1969, Oltmans received a letter from Washington attorney Bernard "Bud" Fensterwald. Well-known in the capital's legal circles, Fensterwald throughout the 1960s was the Chief Counsel for the Senate Judiciary Committee. He had, along with Richard Sprague, founded the private "Committee to Investigate Assassinations". Its primary goal was to look into the Kennedy murder.

In his correspondence, Fensterwald expressed his interest in meeting George de Mohrenschildt and asked if Oltmans could make the arrangements. And he wanted, if possible, to listen to the tape-recorded interviews with George and Jeanne. He wrote that he had become convinced that de Mohrenschildt was a key figure in a conspiracy and plot orchestrated to assassinate the President, and for that reason he felt it was vital that he review the recordings.

Oltmans' notes revealed that Fensterwald contacted him at least four times, always making the same requests. At one point, he said, "You're the only one. Willem; you're the one person in the world who holds the key to unraveling the plot that killed John F. Kennedy, due to your close and personal friendship with George de Mohrenschildt."

On March 3, 1975, Oltmans contacted George and mentioned the contacts that he had with Bernard "Bud" Fensterwald. Obviously concerned, de Mohrenschildt angrily instructed Oltmans not to allow him to hear the interview recordings, saying in a loud voice, "I will never meet with this fucking Jew."

Somewhat defensively, Oltmans noted, George brought up the 1500 U. S.-trained Cubans that had been captured in the Bay of Pigs invasion and how in the heat of the battle the Kennedys had cowardly abandoned them to be captured and imprisoned by Castro.

To obtain their freedom, Robert Kennedy had helped to negotiate a deal for 68 million dollars in medical supplies and medications to be sent to the Cuban regime. The Kennedys then let the freed Cubans into the United States, George commented, and each and every one of them would gladly have volunteered to have killed both of the brothers.

Oltmans' notes address his reluctance to deal with Fensterwald. It had taken him years and years to gain the trust of de Mohrenschildt, and he was just now beginning to open up and tell what he knew. Allowing this Washington attorney suddenly to intervene, review all of Oltmans' investigative work and use him as his contact for a personal meeting with George was simply not in the cards.

On May 10, 1976, Oltmans received a letter from George in which he said he had just read an article in the March issue of Time magazine that named Willem Oltmans as possibly being a KGB agent. Amused, de Mohrenschildt wrote, "You will now become the victim of great dark powers."

Oltmans' notes show his anger at being slandered. He referred to the allegation as "pure bullshit", claiming it originated with De Telegraaf - the largest Dutch daily newspaper, with a circulation of over half a million readers. It was known throughout the Netherlands for its willingness to print sensational stories. Oltmans saw that one as just another example of the smear campaign that haunted his journalism career.

Another letter from George in May of 1976 mentioned that Readers Digest had made an offer to pay the couple $4000 for a four-day interview and include the use of a Hertz rental car. The interviewer, Edward J. Epstein, had spoken with the de Mohrenschildts in Dallas and assured them that the story of their relationship with Lee and Marina Oswald would be told fairly and truthfully.

In the initial meeting, George told Willem, Jeanne had done most of the talking and rambled on and on with Epstein. Several days after the interview had been completed, she received a small package in the mail from Epstein. It was a gift of caviar, which Jeanne was thrilled to receive. George found that quite amusing.

1976 would prove to be a pivotal year in the life of George de Mohrenschildt. Returning from a trip to California, he and Jeanne discovered that their Charming Lane apartment had been entered by a person or persons unknown, and an address book was missing. It appeared as though someone had rifled through George's personal files. The incident put the couple on edge, as they had no idea who would do such a thing and what they might be after. This illegal entry would be the beginning of a downward spiral for de Mohrenschildt and his wife, as they became increasingly paranoid.

George would send a handwritten letter on September 5th to George Herbert Walker Bush, then Director of the CIA, pleading for his help in removing the net that "vigilantes" seemed to be tightening around Jeanne and himself. Oltmans took note of the fact that he addressed Bush by his first name, indicating that there was a close friendship between the two men.

Further investigation confirmed that de Mohrenschildt had known Bush since his days at Phillips Academy in Andover, Massachusetts, in 1940. Bush's roommate was Edward Gordon Hooker, and George de Mohrenschildt was Hooker's uncle. But it has been speculated by many that he and Bush had also been long-time associates.

Below is the text of the letter de Mohrenschildt sent to George H. W. Bush:

Dear George,

You will excuse this hand-written letter. Maybe you will be able to bring a solution to the hopeless situation I find myself in.

My wife and I find ourselves surrounded by some vigilantes, our phone bugged, and we are being followed everywhere. Either FBI is involved in this or they do not want to accept my complaints. We are driven to insanity by the situation.

I have been behaving like a damn fool ever since my daughter Nadya died from (cystic fibrosis) over three years ago. I tried to write, stupidly and unsuccessfully, about Lee H Oswald and must have angered a lot of people I do not know. But to punish an elderly man like myself and my highly nervous and sick wife is really too much.

Could you do something to remove the net around us? This will be my last request for help and I will not annoy you any more.

Good luck in your important job.

Thank you so much.

George de Mohrenschildt

And this is the return letter from Bush:

Let me say first that I know it must have been difficult for you to seek my help in the situation outlined in your letter. I believe I can appreciate your state of mind in view of your daughter's tragic death a few years ago, and the current poor state of your wife's health. I was extremely sorry to hear of these circumstances. In your situation I can well imagine how the attentions you described in your letter affect both you and your wife.

However, my staff has been unable to find any indication of interest in your activities on the part of federal authorities in recent years. The flurry of interest that attended your testimony before the Warren Commission has long subsided. I can only speculate that you may have become "newsworthy" again in view of the renewed interest in the Kennedy assassination, and thus may be attracting the attention of people in the media.

I hope this letter had been of some comfort to you, George, although I realize I am unable to answer your question completely.

George Bush, Director of the Central Intelligence Agency.

A close reading of both letters leaves very little doubt that these two men knew each other and were therefore on a first-name basis.

As 1976 drew to a close, Oltmans was on the speaking circuit and had flown into Dallas for a visit with George. But when he landed and called the apartment, Jeanne informed him that her husband was at Parkland Hospital and very ill, suffering the effects of what she described as a nervous breakdown.

In a strange turn of events, an unknown doctor had reportedly visited the de Mohrenschildt apartment and administered intravenous medications. Soon thereafter, de Mohrenschildt's mental state began to deteriorate and hospitalization became necessary.

Later, on May 11, 1978, the Fort Worth <u>Evening Star</u> had tried to develop information regarding the mysterious visitor. But nothing was found, and to this day he has not been identified. Subsequently, George was to make five separate unsuccessful attempts to commit suicide. He was being treated by Doctor Charles Mendoza, a new physician who had been in Dallas for only two months. Jeanne had signed George into the hospital's mental health ward under his care.

At their last meeting, Willem had confronted Jeanne about her jealousy and domineering ways and had stormed out of the apartment, promising never to return. In a surprising phone call, she asked that he come to visit her. But he was in the city just for a stopover and needed to leave right away for New York. He said he'd be returning in a few months, when George hopefully would be out of the hospital.

Once that phone conversation had ended, Willem called Pat Russell to ask about George's condition and hospitalization. He learned that de Mohrenschildt had been receiving shock treatments but was to be released that very morning and could meet for a lunch date at the Cipango Club. Oltmans' notes indicate that he was both shocked and suspicious upon hearing this news. He wondered if in fact Pat Russell and Jeanne were conspiring to keep George from telling what he knew concerning President Kennedy's assassination and from going through with the publication of his book I Am A Patsy, I Am A Patsy.

The reader may recall that at an earlier lunch meeting, Russell had warned Oltmans to be very careful in releasing any material from de Mohrenschildt's manuscript, saying, "I don't know what all the man knows; it's a very fishy affair! If he spills the whole goddamn thing. he'll go straight to jail".

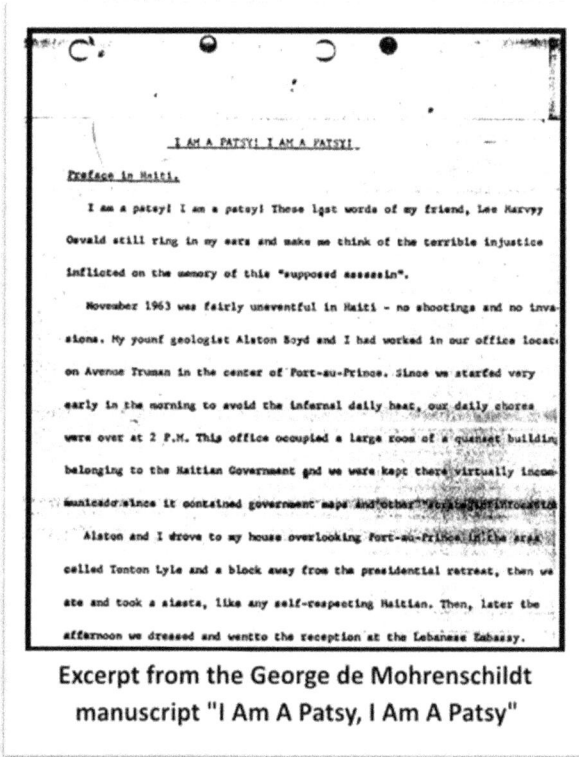

I AM A PATSY! I AM A PATSY!

Preface in Haiti.

I am a patsy! I am a patsy! Those last words of my friend, Lee Harvey Oswald still ring in my ears and make me think of the terrible injustice inflicted on the memory of this "supposed assassin".

November 1963 was fairly uneventful in Haiti - no shootings and no invasions. My younf geologist Alston Boyd and I had worked in our office located on Avenue Truman in the center of Port-au-Prince. Since we started very early in the morning to avoid the infernal daily heat, our daily chores were over at 2 P.M. This office occupied a large room of a quonset building belonging to the Haitian Government and we were kept there virtually incommunicado since it contained government maps and other material ...

Alston and I drove to my house overlooking Port-au-Prince in the area called Tonton Lyle and a block away from the presidential retreat, then we ate and took a siesta, like any self-respecting Haitian. Then, later the afternoon we dressed and wentto the reception at the Lebanese Embassy.

Excerpt from the George de Mohrenschildt manuscript "I Am A Patsy, I Am A Patsy"

As usual, the Cipango Club was abuzz with the conversations of the city's upper crust. Pat Russell, his lover Greg and George de Mohrenschildt were already seated when Willem Oltmans arrived. Charismatic and suave, the Dutch journalist moved through the oversize dining room with the ease of a local politician - shaking hands, patting backs and giving broad smiles from table to table. Standing to meet him, George appeared healthy and fit. With a strong handshake and a hug, the two old friends were reunited.

As always, Russell took the lead and tried to control the seating arrangement so de Mohrenschildt was not next to Willem. But his efforts failed, as Oltmans forced his way to the chair right beside George. The conversation at the table quickly moved from one topic to another. His notes revealed that Willem was shocked by how George, when speaking, appeared nervous and tense and very much unlike his usual confident self. Minutes into the luncheon, he leaned in and whispered to Oltmans in French that he needed to speak with him privately and that it was urgent.

The whispering appeared to make Pat Russell uneasy. His eyes darted from one face to the other. It was clear that he was uncomfortable being left out of the conversation. Finally, he asked Willem how would he like his young lover Greg to show him around Dallas and even take him to the sauna at the Dallas Club.

Without even a moment of thought, Oltmans rejected the offer and said that instead he would take a ride with George. Still not over his discomfort, and clearly dissatisfied, Russell stared at both men quietly for a moment as he took a long draw on a cigarette. Conversation had ceased. As the lunch meeting ended, he gave George one last long look and walked out in silence, with Greg in tow.

CHAPTER SIXTEEN

Oltmans left with de Mohrenschildt in his friend's new gray Pinto. As they drove away, he recorded in his notes that George appeared uneasy and visibly shaken. "They're trying to ruin my memory," he said. "You mean from the shock treatments at the hospital?" Willem asked. In a soft voice, George replied, "It's time now. I must tell you this. Let's go to a private place so we can talk at ease."

They wound through the streets of Dallas, and Oltmans couldn't help wondering if the moment of truth had finally arrived. Would George reveal what he had held so close to his chest all those years regarding his influence over Lee Harvey Oswald? Oltmans saw that they were approaching the Bishop College campus, and de Mohrenschildt suggested that they go to a quiet corner spot in the Zale Library.

It was February 23, 1977. At a simple wooden table with two rather plain chairs, surrounded by bookcases, Willem Oltmans' years of effort culminated in a simple but earth-shaking statement.

With tears welling in his eyes, George spoke in a voice that was barely louder than a whisper. "Willem," he began, "I feel responsible for the actions of Lee Harvey Oswald. I directed Lee Oswald and he followed my directions. And because of that direction, I was involved the assassination of President Kennedy. What do you think will happen to me if I admit this?"

It seemed to Oltmans that time stood still as both men sat in total silence. "Why are you just now telling me this?" he asked. "I trust you," de Mohrenschildt replied. "It is now time that I tell the truth. The whole world already writes scandalous things about me."

Dropping his head and continuing in a sad, soft voice, he said, "Willem, my wife has left me and will never return. Bishop College has informed me that my contract will not be renewed. I'm 65 years old. I'm at the end of a long journey."

As Willem tried to absorb this incredible admission, his mind raced back to February 2, 1967, when in the office of Carel Enkelaar at NOS Television, Gerard Croiset had outlined his incredibly clear vision of a man behind the actions of Lee Harvey Oswald and the assassination of President Kennedy. It was all proving to be true. The Amazing Dutchman had been right.

Zale Library, Bishop College

Oltmans knew it was the greatest story of his career. It would be Willem Oltmans, The Netherlands' globetrotting master of journalism, who had dug up this hidden part of history - the real story behind the assassination of President John F. Kennedy - and would present it for all the world to hear. As the two men sat eyeing each other, there was little left to say. Soon, they got up to leave.

As they departed the Library, George began to express his concerns that he was being stalked and might even be poisoned. Willem rushed for the nearest phone, where he placed a call to Carel Enkelaar to report the admission by George de Mohrenschildt and his fears for his safety.

Enkelaar instructed Oltmans to get de Mohrenschildt to The Netherlands as fast as possible – regardless of the cost - so they could get his statement on film. Hearing that all expenses for the trip would be paid and NOS Television would assist in finding a publisher for his manuscript, George agreed to the arrangements. "I will go," he said. "I must go. I just must tell the truth."

Now, for the first time, real fear had gripped both men. Rushing from one step to the next, Oltmans knew that the accomplishing the task ahead would require the ultimate in perseverance. Getting George to The Netherlands and breaking the story would take all the ingenuity the seasoned Dutch journalist could muster.

First, de Mohrenschildt would need to close all of his bank accounts and withdraw his retirement savings at Bishop College. But as they pulled up and parked at Oak Cliff Bank and Trust Company, George lost his nerve and refused to go further. He then began to vacillate, telling Oltmans he wasn't sure he could follow through with his promise to tell all he knew. After a few minutes of reflection, he did leave the car. But he came right back, still trying to convince himself that he could do what was required of him.

Finally, de Mohrenschildt was able to enter the bank, obtain his funds and have the cash converted to $100 United States Travelers Checks. Upon returning to his cramped apartment on campus, he canceled his medical insurance. He now had about $4600 in liquid assets.

Still quite upset, George predicted that "they" would never allow him to depart the country. He pleaded with Willem not to leave him alone – even for a minute. And he began to describe several strange occurrences in the last few weeks that had fueled his concern.

There had been several times, he said, when he had parked his car at Bishop College, only to return and find it gone. It would then turn up near another building on campus. "Could it possible be that you just forgot where you had parked it?" Willem asked. George replied that he was certain where he had left the vehicle.

He also spoke of a woman who lived across from his residence and appeared to be observing his every move. "If I come in, she's there watching. If I leave, she's there watching. When I look out my window, I see her peeking from behind her curtain. There she is, watching," he said. Listening to all this, Willem found himself wondering if the stories were simply a product of George's paranoia. But soon, he was to have the very same experience.

After a restless night during which he barely slept, de Mohrenschildt suggested that they return to the privacy of the Zale Library, where they could safely make their plans. As the two men entered, Oltmans had occasion to witness George's strong attachment to his students – several of whom stopped to speak with him. Viewing that previously unseen side of his now-troubled friend brought him great comfort.

Soon they were alone once again at that same corner table where just the day before George had made his startling statements. The two men began to discuss exactly how and when they would leave for The Netherlands.

Once again, de Mohrenschildt showed signs of uncertainty that he would successfully make his escape. "They will never allow me to leave Dallas," he proclaimed, "much less leave the country." "You have a current passport, don't you?" Willem asked. "Yes, but they will never allow me to leave," George repeated.

Oltmans pressed him for specifics. "Who is 'they'?" he inquired. Matter-of-factly, de Mohrenschildt replied, "The enemy. Everyone who doesn't want the truth about the Kennedy assassination to come out. And the Jewish Mafia. They've been after me for years."

When the men left the library, they walked to where George's car had been parked. But it was not there. Now Oltmans began to realize that something strange was indeed going on. Taking a short walk around the campus, they located the Pinto in an area adjacent to an entirely different building. And there was more.

In the front seat, someone had left a warning: "We know where you are. We know how to find you. Beware!"

Oltmans' notes tell of the deep fear they both felt at that point. He told George, "We must get out of here as fast as possible." During the slow drive back to George's apartment, they thought of what now had to be done – the story that had to be told.

Feeling exhausted, Willem reflected upon the fact that his ten-year friendship and journey of discovery was now coming to fruition. What had begun with de Mohrenschildt's denial of any kind of involvement had led to a revelation of what was quite likely the truth. It was as if a great wall of secrecy had finally crumbled.

CHAPTER SEVENTEEN

George spoke of his concern that any admission of guilt on his part for mentoring and influencing Lee Harvey Oswald would have a negative effect upon his daughter and his brother. He said, "I would rather kill myself than have my family live the rest of their lives being tied to this event through my actions." Oltmans' notes mention his belief that de Mohrenschildt wanted to unburden himself and tell what really had happened in Dallas but thought he would be risking incarceration by doing so.

"Do you know what it is like to be imprisoned all alone?" he asked. "It's my fear if I come out now and tell the real truth, I'll surely be imprisoned. How can I tell the real truth and not be imprisoned?" In truth, Oltmans felt that George would likely be tried and convicted and end up behind bars...or might even be executed.

Regarding his time with Dr. Mendoza, he said, "I was drugged and threatened." The notes tell of George's deep concern that Jeanne and Pat Russell had conspired against him and arranged for the commitment to Parkland Hospital against his will. He referred to them as his worst enemies and said he had long suspected the two would do anything to keep him from revealing all he knew concerning the assassination of President Kennedy.

Indeed, what Willem had heard about the hospital stay had led him to conclude that something very strange and unusual had gone on there. George was convinced that the shock treatments were administered in an attempt to alter his memory.

Wavering once again in regard to making the trip to The Netherlands, de Mohrenschildt considered backing out of his commitment to tell the whole truth once and for all. At one point, he told Willems, "We must leave right now at this moment or I will change my mind." Pacing back and forth in the small room, George was clearly a torn and tortured soul, well aware that he was making a life-altering decision.

"My God... I'm burning my bridges," he told Oltmans, who sat quietly, watching and listening. The apartment was in complete disarray, with clothes strewn everywhere, half-eaten plates of food left to rot and what appeared to be a very large, razor-sharp machete lying within inches of his nightstand. Finally, de Mohrenschildt took two suitcases from a small closet and began to gather his belongings from the floor and stuff them in.

He slammed the tops closed and paused to take one more look at the little sanctuary where he had spent his last days at Bishop College. In Willem Oltmans' notes, he tells of his feeling that George would not be returning to Dallas. All of his actions were those of someone who was making arrangements never to come back.

As the two men exited the apartment, the door directly across from George's opened. And there was the strange neighbor he had described as spying on him ever since he moved in. They all stood motionless, staring at each other. Finally Willem spoke, asking the middle-aged woman, "Do we have something of yours?" Looking at him steely-eyed, she replied that she was waiting for someone. It was one o'clock in the morning.

As they continued their walk to the car, she never moved and continued to watch their every move until the car pulled away. "Now do you see what I had told you about her?" George asked. "If I enter, she's there. If I leave, she's there. Always the same cold-eyed stare, never saying a word. I have an idea she even tried to poison me. My morning milk would be delivered to my front door, and on one occasion after drinking the milk, I became very ill. And that very morning as I got the milk from the front doorway, there she was standing and watching. I never drank the milk again."

They drove through the streets of downtown Dallas, heading for the freeway and, ultimately, escape to Houston. The sidewalks were empty, and occasionally they passed a taxi waiting for a call. Glancing over his shoulder from time to time, George appeared to be wondering if it was finally over. In a strange way, Willem noted, he seemed relieved to be leaving it all behind. Surely the weight of one of the darkest moments in United States history had been a difficult burden to bear for all those years.

The city skyline soon diminished to a glow in the rear view mirror. They were well underway, driving along a lonely Texas highway. Willem mentioned to de Mohrenschildt that if Lee Oswald had been the person who was used in the assassination of President Kennedy, he must have been paid a large sum of money. In a very calm and low voice, George replied, "Lee never lived long enough to receive the money."

Feeling that the time was right, Oltmans asked George again if he had known Jack Ruby. Without hesitation, he said, "Yes, I knew Jack Ruby." For the entire ten years they had been associated with each other, de Mohrenschildt had always denied knowing Oswald's killer.

In an even more startling revelation, he told Oltmans that he had left Haiti and returned to Dallas only a short time before President Kennedy's assassination had taken place and then had returned to Haiti before it was carried out. In that very unguarded moment in the car, George had begun to open up.

At about four A.M., the weary men stopped at The Hunters Lodge Motel, a few miles outside of Houston, and checked in for the remainder of the night.

One must wonder what de Mohrenschildt and Oltmans were thinking as they lay there, sharing that small room in the early morning hours. Would the story that they were about to release unleash a media firestorm throughout America and the world? Would this be the downfall of one of the most mysterious individuals connected to the events of November 22, 1963? Would it mean achieving the journalistic glory Willem Oltmans had so passionately sought throughout his career?

After only a few hours of sleep, they continued their drive into Houston. Arriving at around nine A.M., the two checked into a Holiday Inn only minutes from the city's airport. George had a few things left to do before their departure for New York. He arranged for David Russell, an old friend who managed Polo's Restaurant in Houston, to come and take the Ford Pinto for safekeeping until his return.

He then phoned Bishop College, announced his plans for a European trip and told them that his campus apartment was empty. Finally, he called Reader's Digest to inform them that he would not be back in the United States until at least March 15, 1977, for his four-day interview.

At 12 Noon, the two men left Houston via Braniff Airlines. Somewhat more relaxed, George complained about the meal that had been served in the first class section of the plane. As he and Willem sat side-by-side sipping white wine, he said, "You've saved my life. You do know that." It was the first of several times that he would make that same statement.

CHAPTER EIGHTEEN

After they arrived at New York's Kennedy Airport, they checked into the Waldorf Astoria Hotel – sharing a room, at de Mohrenschildt's insistence. Arrangements for their flight to London were being ironed out by NOS Television. After a misunderstanding with KLM, they had two tickets in hand for seats aboard a Pan American flight.

It was a momentous step toward getting George to The Netherlands and in front of the NOS cameras. Departure would be at ten A.M. the next day – March 2, 1977. They took advantage of the opportunity to spend some time in Manhattan. Riding in the taxi, both of them were lost in their own thoughts and memories of previous exploits in the city.

After enjoying an early room service breakfast, they headed for the airport, arriving just in time to board the Pan Am jumbo jetliner. George and Willem settled into their first class seats for the long transatlantic flight to London. Oltmans recorded in his notes that the trip was uneventful and that George seemed relaxed and completely at ease.

Upon their arrival in London, Willem called Carel Enkelaar, who was shocked to hear that he was in London and had George de Mohrenschildt with him. "I just can hardly believe it," Enkelaar said. "God bless you, Willem. You have really done a wonderful job, and let me tell you all of us here know it."

Leaving the airport In a taxi, Oltmans directed the driver to The Hotel Britannia. He noticed that George's demeanor had changed once again. He seemed depressed and moody. "We must share the same room at the Britannia," de Mohrenschildt urged. Trying to ease his mind, Willem agreed. He further recommended that they go and visit his long-time friend and companion Peter Van de Wouw, who was performing at the Phoenix Theater.

By the time the three got together, George had calmed down. Looking directly into Peter's eyes and with both hands on his shoulders, he said, "Willem saved my life. I'm forever indebted to him." But as the evening wound down and they arrived at the hotel, he was once again sullen and depressed and doubted he would be able to sleep. Oltmans' notes describe him as tossing and turning for hours, perhaps tortured by his thoughts.

And so it was time to arrange the final leg of their journey to The Netherlands. Willem made reservations for seats on a British Airways flight to Amsterdam. But once they were airborne high above the North Sea, George suddenly lost his composure. He jumped to his feet and began asking other passengers why his ticket was for just a one-way flight. That wasn't the case, but de Mohrenschildt refused to accept anyone's confirmation that he in fact did have a round-trip reservation.

With a wild look in his eyes, George was frantic as he paced up and down the aisle of the plane. Passengers were becoming nervous, and the group fell totally silent. With his voice rising, de Mohrenschildt was by now entering a full state of panic, and the cabin crew rushed to try to console him. Finally, the head stewardess came and patiently explained that his ticket was for a full round trip and did include return travel to Houston.

Shocked and amazed by George's outburst, Willem felt that he was going off the deep end right there on the airplane. It was as if de Mohrenschildt had been drugged, he recorded. Still completely out of control, George continued to insist that his ticket was for only one way. "Look at your ticket more closely, George," Willem, now agitated, told him. "You promised me a return ticket to Houston and it's not on here," George insisted. Oltmans said, "But it *is* on there, George. Now sit down and calm down."

The remainder of the flight was marked by stares and whispers, as their fellow passengers wondered what to make of de Mohrenschildt's performance. When they arrived at Schiphol airport in Amsterdam, the passengers began to exit. But George remained seated. "I refuse to leave this plane," he proclaimed. "I will not get off this plane until I have a return ticket to Houston, Texas."

With no one left aboard except for the flight staff and them, an exasperated Willem leaned down, looked George right in the eye and in a very stern voice said, "Get up out of that seat and get off of this airplane."

Without saying another word, de Mohrenschildt rose, gathered his bag and disembarked. It had been an embarrassing incident, Oltmans wrote in his notes, but he couldn't help feeling pity for his friend. In the terminal, they went to the KLM Airlines counter to confirm that George did indeed have a round-trip ticket.

During the taxi ride into Amsterdam on their way to Peter Van de Wouw's apartment, de Mohrenschildt gazed out the window and spoke of how the Dutch people seemed so prosperous and content in comparison to Americans. "Do you think Europe is more beautiful than America?" Willem asked. George replied, "Well, you know very well my anti-Americanism."

By the time they arrived, he seemed at ease again. Dinner was set for that evening at a local restaurant, and then they would be driving to Utrecht and the home of Gerard Croiset. The long-awaited meeting between the two was finally going to take place. It was in February of 1967 that Croiset had first told of his intense vision of the architect behind the assassination.

George sat silently and appeared to be somewhat tense as they drove to the Croiset residence. Both Gerard Croiset and Carel Enkelaar met them at the door. Croiset spoke almost no English and greeted the visitors in Dutch. As he and de Mohrenschildt stood face-to-face, Willem was overtaken by an almost eerie sensation. Then, Croiset gently lifted his hands to a position right above George's head and began to move them in a slow, circular pattern.

The effect upon de Mohrenschildt was immediate. "What an incredible feeling I have just had," he said. "I have never in my life felt so relaxed and calm. I have never felt the feeling of such pleasure. What wonderful, powerful hands you have." Without touching George's head, Croiset told the group that he had damage to the right side of his skull.

In utter amazement, de Mohrenschildt responded, "Yes, as a child I dove once into a half-full swimming pool and damaged the right side of my head. This is truly incredible." As the evening passed, he said very little but watched and listened intently. Croiset offered to treat him every day he was in The Netherlands, in order for him to achieve complete calmness and inner peace.

It had been agreed that they would meet the following day at the offices of Strengholt Publishing Company to discuss the publication of George's book I Am A Patsy, I Am A Patsy. On the way there, he was cheerful and upbeat and hoped they would like his work. As the group sat and discussed the possibilities, the Strengholt executive asked to see the written manuscript.

"It's still in the files of my Dallas attorney, Pat Russell," de Mohrenschildt said. Somewhat annoyed that it had not been brought along on the flight, the executive asked how fast the material could be delivered. He stated that they were prepared to offer a contract - and if this project were to go forward, they would need to have the manuscript.

Willem stood and walked to the office telephone, where he placed a call to Pat Russell's law office and described the situation. The attorney's reaction was unexpected. "Well, we need to talk about this now," Russell said. "My client, Jeanne de Mohrenschildt, has some rights to that material, and we would have to have an agreement and come to terms before we could ever release the manuscript."

Agitated by the turn of events, Willem snapped, "Well, we'll have to see what George wants to do." He hung up the phone. Upon hearing the bad news, de Mohrenschildt commented, "Haven't I told you, Willem? Those two – Pat Russell and Jeanne – are my worst enemies. They'll do everything in their power to stop me from telling all that I know." In Oltmans' notes, there's a comment by George regarding his feelings toward Russell. He said he didn't trust him and called him "deviously clever".

Their Stengholt contact offered to put de Mohrenschildt up in a local hotel suite, where he could start writing his memoirs all over again. Shaking his head from side to side, George said, "That may be the only way. Just start all over." Turning and looking directly at Oltmans, George joked, "One day I will take a gun and shoot you, Willem. You will finally get the chance to get everything out of me."

The group sat stunned, and no one spoke. Finally, Oltmans broke the silence, saying, "Okay, you all just heard the threat. Now if something happens to me, you know who did it."

On their way back to the apartment, according to his notes, Willem couldn't help but feel that George was seriously conflicted. He badly wanted to confess his involvement and tell all he knew concerning the Kennedy murder but was very frightened of implicating himself and of the long-lasting effects his actions would have on him and his family. He noticed that de Mohrenschildt seemed lost in deep thought during the drive. After much subsequent discussion, a contract was offered to George to tell his story. The signing date would be March 8, 1977.

CHAPTER NINETEEN

O n March 5, Oltmans noted, a short road trip was planned. It was to be a one-day journey to Brussels. On the way back, Willem thought de Mohrenschildt might like to see his old school, the University of Liege, where he had received his Doctorate of Science in International Commerce in 1938. George had not been in Belgium for over twenty years.

A lunch date at the Hotel Metropole had been arranged with a friend of Willem's - a Soviet diplomat by the name of Vladimir Kuznyetsov. It should be mentioned that First Secretary Kouznyetsov was the former head of the KGB in The Netherlands.

Arriving early, Willem and George left the car in the hotel parking garage and decided to make a stop to get some postcards before heading to the dining room. As they were leaving the gift shop, Kuznyetsov suddenly appeared. He spoke directly to George in Russian, which Oltmans didn't understand. It was apparent that they knew one another.

The tone of the brief conversation was firm and direct. Only seconds after the last words were exchanged, George announced that he was going to take a short walk and meet the other two in an hour or less in the dining room. He walked away with his briefcase in hand and never looked back.

And that was the last time Willem Oltmans saw George de Mohrenschildt alive.

More than three hours passed, and Willem and Kuznyetsov were left wondering what had happened. Oltmans told Kuznyetsov that George was prepared to sign a contract in the next few days for publication of a manuscript that revealed his involvement in the John F. Kennedy assassination. "This is very, very important," Kuznyetsov said. "You should get everything written down and recorded as soon as possible."

Willem left the hotel and drove around Brussels, hoping that he could spot de Mohrenschildt and convince him to return with him to The Netherlands. After several hours, he gave up and headed back to Amsterdam alone. Rushing into the apartment, Oltmans found all of George's personal belongings still lying right where they had been that morning before the two men departed for Brussels. Everything had been left behind – his pipe, his clothes, even his toothbrush.

As Willem sat alone in the apartment, he couldn't help but think that something strange had happened. George had been in an upbeat mood and seemed to have calmed down. He was ready to sign his contract in the next several days, and then suddenly he was gone. You don't just leave all that you have and disappear into thin air. Did It have something to do with what was said when de Mohrenschildt met Kuznyetsov?

Having been gone for over two decades, he supposedly knew no one in Belgium. Where would he go? Concerned that he might have been harmed, Oltmans called Carel Enkelaar and informed him of the situation. He was advised not to contact the authorities right away and to wait a day or two and see if George reappeared on his own.

On Monday, March 7, there was still no trace of de Mohrenschildt. Enkelaar instructed Willem to notify the American Embassies in Brussels and The Hague that an American citizen was missing. After that, all he could do was to wait at the apartment for the phone to ring or someone to knock on the door. Now gripped by nervousness and fear, Oltmans kept replaying in his mind George's statement that he had not been in the country for more than twenty years.

Then, as evening approached, he received a very strange phone call from an individual who identified himself only as "Mr. Genta". The caller said he was calling from Brussels on behalf of his friend George de Mohrenschildt, who had directed him to go to Amsterdam and collect his personal belongings. In addition, he was to inform Willem that George had returned to the United States.

Oltmans replied angrily that he would never release de Mohrenschildt's personal belongings to anyone other than George himself, and if he wanted them back he must come in person to retrieve them. Willem told the person that everything George had left in Amsterdam was now stored safely in a local bank depository.

In his notes, he reported that the mysterious caller had a very strong, distinct Middle Eastern accent. Years later, he would express his regret at not having "Mr. Genta" come to Amsterdam so he could meet the so-called "friend" of de Mohrenschildt.

Oltmans advised American Embassy Press Official Jacob Gillespie in Brussels and Ambassador Robert J.McClusky at the American Embassy in The Hague that George was not missing, and that he was back in the United States.

On the morning of March 8, 1977, Willem made a call to Robert Tanenbaum, the Chief Counsel to the House Select Committee on Assassinations in Washington, to talk about his friendship with George de Mohrenschildt and his findings. Tanenbaum was a former New York City District Attorney for Manhattan, well-known for his fierce courtroom tactics and having never lost a felony trial during his time in the position.

During Oltmans' initial contact with him on February 11, 1977, he, Ken Klein and Cliff Fenton had tried to get the details of Willem's close friendship with de Mohrenschildt and what he information he had gleaned from it. But they were left with the feeling that the journalist had been less than forthcoming and wasn't revealing some important details.

This time, the conversation with Tanenbaum was crucial, and Oltmans knew it.

He explained that de Mohrenschildt had come to The Netherlands and had an appointment to finalize a publishing contract for his story regarding his involvement in the John F. Kennedy assassination but had disappeared in Brussels the day before the signing was to occur. Hearing of this new development, Tanenbaum said he wanted Oltmans to testify before the Committee as soon as possible. The bombshell that Willem had just dropped had the potential to change history. It could very well have been the "smoking gun" that America and the world had awaited for so long. and Robert Tanenbaum knew it. Oltmans agreed to appear at 10 A.M. on Tuesday, March 15, in Room 2318 of the Sam Rayburn House Office Building and to bring all of his documentation.

On March 9, he received an urgent telegram from Tanenbaum asking that any filmed material that NOS Television had concerning de Mohrenschildt also be brought for the committee's investigation. NOS agreed to send along the nine hours of tapes that were recorded with both Jeanne and George de Mohrenschildt back in 1969.

As word began to spread throughout The Netherlands that Willem Oltmans had crucial evidence concerning the JFK assassination, all of the major media turned the spotlight on the Dutch journalist. He was besieged by phone calls and requests for interviews but was selective and spoke to only a few Dutch outlets.

He chose NCRV Television, one of The Netherlands' most prominent stations, to release a small statement concerning his findings. All it said was that Oltmans had become personal friends with a man named George de Mohrenschildt from Dallas, Texas, whom he named as a "very big fish" involved in the assassination of President John F. Kennedy - and he could not comment further at that time, considering that de Mohrenschildt had mysteriously disappeared only days before while attending a meeting in Brussels.

Meanwhile, NOS Television phone lines were ringing non-stop. The story was bigger than any they had ever been involved with. The results of the ten-year-long investigation that had led to a close personal friendship between Willem Oltmans and George de Mohrenschildt would soon be revealed to the world.

In those first few days after George had disappeared, Willem knew he needed to accelerate the process to release his findings and relate all that de Mohrenschildt had said. It was now or never. No matter the outcome, the truth had to be told. And Willem Oltmans was determined to tell it.

While still in The Netherlands and preparing for his appearance before the House Select Committee, Oltmans received a call from the American Embassy in Den Haag, confirming that George de Mohrenschildt had been located in the United States. Later, he would learn that George had stayed in Europe for ten days at an undisclosed location before flying back to America.

The "Mr. Genta" who had phoned Oltmans trying to retrieve de Mohrenschildt's belongings was never heard from again and remains a mystery even today.

CHAPTER TWENTY

The night before Willem was to leave for Washington to testify, he and Carel Enkelaar huddled for one last review of how NOS Television wanted his findings to be laid out for the investigating committee. The two men were in total agreement that all of the material that had been gathered and recorded relative to the de Mohrenschildts would be made available and nothing would be held back.

As soon as Oltmans had checked into the Washington Hilton Hotel on Connecticut Avenue, the phone began ringing. The first call was from CBS Washington correspondent Jim McManus, requesting an in-room interview concerning his upcoming appearance before the assassination committee. He agreed to it but was very guarded in his responses, disclosing as little as possible to the reporter.

After McManus left, Oltmans sat alone for a while, wondering what the following day would bring. It had taken ten years to reach this point. And all along, he had wanted it to be George who would tell the story. It was Willem Oltmans, the investigative journalist, who had discovered it. He was the person who brought de Mohrenschildt to The Netherlands to get him on film. It was his job. It was what he did for a living. This was his bread and butter.

George was to be the one who would correct the historical record, but it wasn't going to happen that way now. There was nothing left for Oltmans to do but reveal everything he knew and let the chips fall where they might.

Oltmans remembered what New Orleans District Attorney Jim Garrison and author Mark Lane had said about what would happen if he ever suggested an alternative to the narrative that America and the world had been fed by the Warren Commission.

The official story was that Lee Harvey Oswald was no more than a disgruntled lone wolf who had murdered John F. Kennedy with no assistance and no influence from anyone or any group. He was warned that his findings would be picked apart and that the American media would go into high gear trying to discredit him. And his personal life would be made fodder for public consumption and dissected and called into question at every turn.

Appearing before the Committee, the charismatic Oltmans presented a chronicle of the events that transpired from February 23, 1977, in Dallas - the day George de Mohrenschildt disclosed his personal involvement in a conspiracy to assassinate President John F. Kennedy - up until George's vanishing from Brussels on March 5. Confident and professional in demeanor but somewhat reserved in his responses to questions, he was, as he later noted, a bit cautious because he wanted to feel out the committee members before he revealed all that he knew.

When it was over, Oltmans came away relieved and certain that his findings and disclosures would be treated fairly and would open new avenues for the Committee's investigation.

Immediately following the hearing, Oltmans recorded that he felt vindicated by Robert Tanenbaum's remarks moments after the committee had adjourned to media outlets all across America and the international news representatives. He had said, "Willem Oltmans gave this committee unique, new and confidential information." But that feeling of self-satisfaction would be short-lived.

One of the many calls Oltmans received after that initial appearance before the Select Committee was from Jim McManus, who wanted a second interview, to be filmed at the CBS studios. As was the normal procedure, he asked how CBS handled the usual honorarium that accompanied an appearance before their cameras. An honorarium is a fee paid in a volunteer capacity or for services for which fees are not traditionally required. An example would be the payment to a guest speaker to cover travel, accommodations, and preparation time.

McManus removed himself from any discussion concerning the subject and referred Willem to executive producer Sanford Socolow, who Oltmans found was "too busy" to discuss honoraria. Willem attempted to explain to Socolow that the material he would lay out before the CBS cameras was the product of a ten-year-long investigation. It included many hundreds of notes and letters and would require a great deal of preparation time.

Oltmans knew that his inquiry concerning compensation was not unusual for a freelance reporter. They made their living by being paid for investigating leads. And Willem's decade-long effort had finally evolved into a major international story. But the CBS executive seemed reluctant to consider an honorarium at all, so Oltmans dropped the subject entirely and agreed to the on-camera session. It lasted for over an hour, and in the end he was paid nothing for doing it.

During the interview, McManus asked Oltmans, "If George de Mohrenschildt indeed confessed that he was behind Lee Harvey Oswald and had instructed him on how to set up the assassination of President Kennedy, why did you not go immediately to the nearest police station and report his claim to the authorities?" Immediately sensing that a finger of accountability was being pointed at him, Willem felt annoyed and disrespected.

In his defense, he responded that he was working as a freelance reporter for NOS Television of Hilversum in The Netherlands, and it had been his intention to bring de Mohrenschildt before their cameras as soon as possible. Later, Oltmans recorded in his private notes that the tension between the two journalists had been palpable. In the days that followed, he would sit for more interviews with NOS Radio, the <u>Fort Worth Star-Telegram</u>, the <u>Washington Star</u> and other media entities.

Surprisingly, CBS News never aired the McManus segment, and none of the other news outlets used their recorded material, either. The long de Mohrenschildt investigation by Oltmans that had finally been brought to light now had been relegated to storage room shelves. It was becoming clear to him that something was going on behind the scenes.

Oltmans said in his notes that he had a strong feeling that American news people felt great jealousy and animosity regarding him and his work. Someone from The Netherlands uncovering the inside story of George de Mohrenschildt and his connections to one of the most horrific acts in recent history had created bad feelings among a large group of American journalists. The crafty Dutchman had worked his way into the heart of the crime of the century, when his American counterparts couldn't even crack the surface.

Leaving Washington for San Francisco, Oltmans had resolved to continue with his speaking engagements and try to move beyond the George de Mohrenschildt investigation. But that was not to be. He received a call from David Russell in Houston, the man who had been given George's Ford Pinto for safe keeping. Russell told him that de Mohrenschildt was now in Manalapan, in Palm Beach County, Florida. He was staying at the home of a Mrs. Charles Tilton III.

George had insisted that he contact Willem and relay to him that he missed him greatly and was okay and very grateful to him for all he had done to try to help him. He also requested that Oltmans call him in Florida. Willem asked Russell if George had mentioned why he left Brussels so suddenly. He had, and the reason he gave was that he didn't have the courage to go through with what they had planned and was scared and fearful of being arrested and jailed.

Oltmans' notes were very specific concerning this conversation. He stated that he would not call George and that the only thing left for de Mohrenschildt to do was to get in touch with the House Select Committee himself and make arrangements to go before them and tell the truth regarding his involvement with Lee Harvey Oswald.

On Monday morning March 27, 1977, Willem phoned Robert Tanenbaum, informed him that George de Mohrenschildt had reappeared and gave him his location in Florida. Thanking Oltmans for the new information, Tanenbaum said he would be sending one of the Committee's lead investigators, Gaeton Fonzi, to interview de Mohrenschildt and arrange for his appearance in Washington.

What happened next would be a life-changing experience for Willem Oltmans. In his personal notes, he described exactly how it all unfolded.

CHAPTER TWENTY-ONE

On March 30, Oltmans had left for Boston, where several meetings were arranged at Harvard and MIT. While eating breakfast the next day in Harvard Square, he purchased a newspaper. And in the headlines was the reported suicide death of George de Mohrenschildt on March 29, 1977. Stunned by the news, Willem was completely overcome by shock.

After reading the story over and over, he finally gathered himself and rushed to his room at the Harvard House Motel. He placed a call to Carel Enkelaar. By then, Oltmans was running full speed on adrenaline. Enkelaar picked up the phone on the first ring and was relieved to hear Willem's voice. "Where are you and are you safe?" he asked. Word had spread like wildfire that the Dutch journalist was missing, and NOS Television had been swamped with questions.

"I'm perfectly safe in Boston, Massachusetts," Oltmans told Enkelaar, who responded, "There's a worldwide search underway for you right now, and the word on the streets is that you're in danger. The National Enquirer has 14 journalists looking for you right now."

The two men now realized that they needed to move quickly to contact the House Select committee again and this time tell them everything that George had revealed concerning his involvement with Lee Harvey Oswald and the assassination of President Kennedy. The moment they hung up, Oltmans called Robert Tanenbaum and requested that he be allowed to appear the following day and under oath give them all the information that his investigation had uncovered.

Within an hour, Tanenbaum called back to say that the committee would hear Oltmans under oath at 10 A.M. on April 1, which was the very next morning. Throwing his clothes into a suitcase and dashing from the Harvard House Motel out to a waiting taxi, Oltmans was off to the airport and a short American Airlines flight back to the nation's capital.

In his room at the Washington Hilton, the phone began to ring almost non-stop. Requests were pouring in from all over the country. NBC, ABC, CBS, newspapers, and radio stations around the world wanted to hear what Oltmans had to tell. Media outlets that had shelved their interviews with him now rushed to get them on the air and report on what the Dutch journalist had uncovered concerning George de Mohrenschildt.

ABC Television in particular pushed Oltmans hard for a one-on-one interview and promised to give him the air time he needed to tell his story to the American public. They assured Oltmans that the tape would not be broadcast until after his appearance before the House Select Committee. Vic Ratner, the network's long-time congressional correspondent, was chosen to sit down with Oltmans at the network's studios in Washington.

Right away, Ratner began asking why he took the word of a man who had been hospitalized for a mental condition seriously. Seeing the direction the questioning was going to take, Willem took a defensive stance. He responded that Russian dissident Vladimir Bukovsky had spent over eight years in a Russian mental institution but was still interesting enough that the President of The United States invited him to the White House.

Oltmans went on to say that, yes, George de Mohrenschildt had spent time in the Parkland Hospital psychiatric ward - but he had found him to be still very lucid and acting quite normal. "And so," he said to Ratner, "I listened to his story concerning his close friendship with Lee Harvey Oswald and his involvement in President Kennedy's murder. This was no crazy man talking."

He explained that his friendship with George had been formed many years before the hospitalization. And then, feeling that the time was right, Oltmans dropped his bombshell. It caught everyone in the ABC studio off guard and brought complete silence to the set.

He announced that indeed there had been a conspiracy behind President Kennedy's assassination and that NOS Television had the proof on film and had kept it secret for the past eight years. He continued, telling Ratner that a man named Loran Hall had confessed to being offered $50,000 by a Dallas oilman named Lester Logue to participate in a plot to assassinate the President. Dallas oilman H.L. Hunt had been mentioned as being involved.

This disclosure created a sensation as the news spread. All of the major American news outlets were now scrambling to get the story. As the interview ended, Ratner explained somewhat apologetically that it was his job to ask critical questions.

Oltmans replied, "Critical questions are fine, but before you start an interview, you make sure you've done your homework regarding this case. I've done mine, and it's taken ten years to do it." As Willem gathered his notes before leaving, he had the feeling that his comment to Ratner would surely create an enemy - and it did. Leaving the studio, Oltmans now had a taste of what was on the horizon.

Next came longtime NBC radio corespondent Peter Heckes. That interview went more smoothly, and in the end Heckes wanted Oltmans to commit to an exclusive contract with NBC for the story. Cautiously, Oltmans approached the subject of a possible honorarium – mentioning once again his ten-year-long investigation that had made it possible finally to bring the story out.

With in hours of the Heckes interview, Oltmans received a call from Bob Endicott of NBC. It was agreed that he would go directly to NBC television after the House Select Committee hearing and announce his findings concerning George de Mohrenschildt and the John F. Kennedy assassination to a nationwide audience. CBS and ABC had lined up wanting Oltmans first, but it would be NBC that won out.

In Oltmans' private notes, he speaks of the honorarium and mentions that the subject worried him. He didn't want to leave the wrong impression that his only goal was to be paid for his story. What he had already revealed concerning George de Mohrenschildt had caused a tidal wave of new questions and raised the real possibility that the long-awaited smoking gun had finally appeared. A nation watched and waited for more details. What would happen next?

CHAPTER TWENTY-TWO

As the big black Cadillac supplied by ABC Television approached the Rayburn building, there were countless reporters waiting, representing news outlets all over America and the world. It was a feeding frenzy on the sidewalk. Stepping from the car, Oltmans was met by a flurry of flash bulbs, all seemingly going off at the same time. Blinded momentarily, he stopped to regain his footing. Then, with ABC reporter Vic Ratner by his side, he pushed his way through the crowd.

So many questions were being shouted that it was virtually impossible to distinguish one from another. Everyone wanted a statement from Oltmans himself, but the Dutch journalist managed to slip through the huge doors of the Rayburn building without ever saying a word.

Later, he would record that as he made those first few steps inside, he glanced up to see the big oil painting of Sam Rayburn, who looked as if he were standing guard over his House of Representatives. As they headed down the corridor toward the hearing room, there was still another reminder of where they were and whose name the mighty building bore: a six-foot bronze statue of Rayburn in a stately pose, created by Felix de Weldon.

At the appointed time, Oltmans pulled his chair up to the witness table to begin his testimony before the entire House Select Committee on Assassinations. The cavernous hearing room was packed with congressmen and people from the news media. There was a feeling of excitement in the air – a sense that something big was about to unfold.

With the drop of the gavel by the Honorable Richardson Preyer, the hearing was called to order. And Washington, along with the rest of America, braced itself for what was about to transpire.

The well-groomed Willem Oltmans sat up straight, thoroughly prepared and anxious to recount exactly what his long investigation and his close friendship with George de Mohrenschildt had found. After he had been sworn in and taken the oath to tell "the whole truth and nothing but the truth", each member of the committee would have a turn to ask questions.

Only once during the entire hearing did Oltmans feel that the interaction had become tense. That was when Robert Tanenbaum appeared to be annoyed that his witness wasn't giving the committee more details of what he learned from George de Mohrenschildt. It had been Willem's intention to be completely honest and forthcoming, and in his mind that's exactly what he had done. But Tanenbaum just couldn't understand how he could have conducted this ten-year investigation without gathering more incriminating information.

Leaning forward in the witness chair, Oltmans - in his strong Dutch accent but speaking in English - replied that George de Mohrenschildt was a very smart man who had for years worked for intelligence services around the world. He had also become familiar with the inside workings of the gigantic oil industry.

For fifteen years, he had managed to hide the true story behind one of the biggest crimes of the century. And he had managed to evade all questions from the Warren Commission and walk away cleared of any wrongdoing.

In short, Oltmans said, George de Mohrenschildt was a master of evasion. Always staying one step ahead and playing his role in the shadows, he was able – in the end – to outmaneuver everyone. For much of his adult life, he had indeed walked "the razor's edge".

There was silence as Oltmans described the "real" de Mohrenschildt. He talked of his efforts to bring George before the cameras to reveal, at his own pace, what he knew of an assassination plot. And, addressing Tanenbaum directly, he asked, "Why doesn't the committee investigate just what did happen to George de Mohrenschildt that last day in Brussels, Belgium?"

Summing up, Oltmans said he believed that de Mohrenschildt finally had been overwhelmed by his situation and the heavy burden of the secret he had concealed for so many years. And it was his deep fear of being jailed and prosecuted that eventually brought him to the end of his road.

The session lasted for three hours and ten minutes. In Oltmans' notes, he stated that he felt that, for the most part, the members of the select committee had treated him fairly and with respect. As he exited the hearing room, he was met by dozens of news reporters shoving microphones toward him, with questions being shouted and flash bulbs blinding him once again. Everyone wanted a piece of him now.

Later that evening, a Canadian broadcasting company located Oltmans and asked if the story he had told about George de Mohrenschildt was nothing more than a way to make money. And wasn't it true that he had plans to publish it and make as much as possible?

Very annoyed by the accusation, Willem responded testily. "Of course I'll publish my story," he said. "I worked ten years to bring this out, and I'm a freelance journalist. This is how I make my living. Why is it that no one asks Henry Kissinger when he sells his story if he's only doing it to make money?

'The Watergate burglars all sold their stories and no one said a word. Now I come here and bring my findings out and am accused of only doing this to make money." Becoming more and more disgusted, Oltmans finally refused to answer any further questions.

Upon his return to the Hilton, Oltmans began to receive more calls for interviews. NBC wanted him to go one-on-one with Bob Endicott that evening. But, tired and exhausted, he turned them down and instead made a commitment for the following day.

Later, as he was sitting alone in his room, Oltmans began to reflect on the day and ponder his next steps. Idly flipping through the TV channels, he stopped on NBC news, where Bob Endicott happened to be reporting on his Select Committee appearance. Endicott told viewers that Committee Chairman Richardson Preyer had said that Oltmans had provided a great deal of information that would take an a lot of time to track down and that some of it might prove to be untraceable.

Angered by what he perceived to be an attempt to cast doubt on his honesty, Willem got on the phone with NBC News and canceled the next day's interview. When asked why he was suddenly taking that step, he said that the comment seemed to be hostile toward him. With that, he slammed the phone down.

Oltmans did grant several interviews the following day, but each time the subject of him being paid for his story was brought up. Gradually, a picture was being painted of a journalist who was selling out. Again and again, Oltmans insisted that his work concerning George de Mohrenschildt was done not for monetary gain but to reveal the truth behind one of the most heinous crimes of the century.

But in spite of his denials, the narrative seemed to take on a life of its own. Only weeks after his testimony before the Select Committee, The New Yorker magazine published an article calling Oltmans "A Journalist With A Price". The negative things being said and written disgusted him. He was called a "hustler" and even a "gigolo". And within two days of his startling disclosures, all of the media outlets had lost interest entirely. Not one newspaper or network pursued the story any longer.

It was clear to Oltmans now that his investigation had been torpedoed by a massive effort to discredit him and his intentions. In one of the last interviews he granted, the questioner went so far as to bring up his sexual preference. Wasn't it true that he was a homosexual? And hadn't his former wife left him in 1960 due to the fact that he was a homosexual?

Oltmans answered those questions with one of his own: "What on earth do my sexual preference and what went on between my former wife and myself have to do with my friendship with George de Mohrenschildt and my investigation?" No reply was given, and at that point the interview ended. But by that time, Oltmans' anger had reached an entirely new level.

Later, he would reflect once again upon the words of Jim Garrison, who said that if he revealed his findings he would be criticized and discredited and his private life would be made fodder for public consumption. And all of that happened just as he had been warned that it would. Now feeling isolated, Oltmans soon was sitting in his hotel room wondering what, if anything, he should do to continue with his de Mohrenschildt investigation.

CHAPTER TWENTY-THREE

A few days later, Willem received a personal letter from the former lead investigator for the House Select Committee, Richard Sprague, who had been fired from his position. Sprague conveyed to Oltmans that he firmly believed that his investigation concerning de Mohrenschildt was credible and that he was indeed very close to what had really happened behind the scenes relative to the John F. Kennedy assassination.

Richard Sprague

The letter, which is in the Oltmans archives, goes on to suggest that there was a very real possibility that George de Mohrenschildt had been mind-programmed when, in the final months of 1976, he was signed into Parkland Hospital's psychiatric ward because of his "depression". During his stay, he was given intravenous medications, ordered and administered by newly-hired Dr. Charles Mendoza, and a series of electroshock treatments conducted by a Dr. Deloach. who was first cousin to former FBI Assistant Director Cartha "Deke" Deloach.

Sprague told of consulting with an expert in mind control programming as part of his own investigation and learning that there was a high probability of de Mohrenschildt having been subjected to such an effort. He exhibited all of the classic symptoms of post-hypnotic suggestion.

In Sprague's version of events, de Mohrenschildt would first have been drugged so he could be more easily hypnotized. Then, electroshock would be used to produced a pain effect that he would subconsciously associate with having thoughts his tormentors didn't want him to harbor or even remember.

Other signs of George having been manipulated in such a way included his irrational fear of being killed and his firm belief that he was being followed and watched – which, of course, was reinforced by causing suspicious incidents to occur. All of this would have been done in order to make de Mohrenschildt appear to be crazy.

Willem's notes recorded how incredibly frightened and shaken George was after being discharged from the hospital. There are several mentions of the fact that he appeared to have been drugged, along with this quote from de Mohrenschildt at the time: "They're trying to ruin my memory. They don't want me to tell what I know." And right before they left the United States for Europe, George had begged Oltmans to help him get out of the United States before "they" killed him.

When we found the Richard Sprague letter in Oltmans archives, we were at first skeptical that George de Mohrenschildt could have unknowingly been subjected to a mind control program. But our further research on the subject produced some very interesting findings.

In 1977, Congressional hearings were held concerning an agency within the United States Government that had willfully carried out and funded projects that administered to unknowing participants doses of mind-altering chemicals and electroshock therapy.

It had been discovered that In the 1960s and early 1970s, the Central Intelligence Agency (CIA) was operating a mind control program called "Project Artichoke", which later was re-dubbed "Project MKULtra". That involved using drugs and electroshock to alter people's memories and regulate their actions.

The timeline in Oltmans' notes shows that within 60 days of George de Mohrenschildt's personal letter to George H. W. Bush, he was an unwilling patient at Parkland Hospital receiving precisely such treatments. Coincidence or connection?

Sprague went on to speculate in his letter that Pat Russell, de Mohrenschildt's attorney, was quite possibly the go-between and was likely working for the CIA. It was Russell who had George's manuscript locked away in his office. And de Mohrenschildt, after his stay at Parkland, never saw it again. It was Sprague's theory that after de Mohrenschildt was dead, the attorney turned the original tell-all manuscript over to the CIA. They then sanitized it before arranging for submission to the House Select Committee. And the members, of course, then found nothing of value in it.

Richard Sprague's letter describes a breakdown in the Select Committee, marked by in-fighting and financial shortfalls that almost kept it from beginning its work. He told Oltmans that the whole thing was a farce and little more than a big show staged for the public's consumption.

Directions were being passed down through the ranks to produce sensational headlines or risk being shut down.

After he had been fired from the Committee staff, Sprague - along with many others who had eagerly anticipated rooting out the truth behind the Kennedy assassination - could do little more than shake his head. Finally, a real murder investigation was to be conducted and Richard Sprague and his hand-picked staff would hit the streets the old-fashioned way and turn over every rock until the whole sorry plot had been laid bare.

And then, just as quickly as it had started, it was over. The gutsy, long-time Philadelphia prosecutor was off the case. Many observers at the time wondered if that development spelled the end of any serious effort to find the facts. Replacing Sprague was G. Robert Blakey, Chief Counsel and Staff Director. There would be fewer people and major cuts to the budget – leaving limited resources that would make any search for the truth considerably more difficult.

In Oltmans' notes, he speaks of his great admiration for Richard Sprague and his appreciation for the information and moral support he had provided.

Willem also recorded his thoughts on the death of George de Mohrenschildt. He spoke of how hard it was to believe and of his deep sadness and his strong affection for his friend. Even though George had spoken many times of taking his own life, Oltmans never believed he would actually do it.

But revealing his role in the conspiracy would surely have resulted in his prosecution and imprisonment – a prospect which terrified de Mohrenschildt. He had said many times that he would rather face death by his own hand than to force his daughter and brother to spend the remainder of their lives knowing of his involvement in President Kennedy's assassination.

March 29, 1977, was the final day of George de Mohrenschildt's life. We can only speculate what might have happened.

We know it was crisp and cool as the sun rose over the Atlantic that morning. George lived in Manalapan, a little oceanside town in Palm Beach County, 55 miles north of Miami Beach. The homes in his area were, by most standards, considered to be mansions.

At 1780 South Ocean Shore Boulevard, the main house was a large, frame structure with an outbuilding at the rear that included a small apartment above a multiple-car garage. The home was equipped with an elevator.

The grounds were stately and well-manicured, with a high privacy hedge in the front that lent the property the look of a compound sitting directly across the street from the Atlantic Ocean. It was the sun-baked, south Florida beachside home of Charles and Nancy Tilton.

In 1942, De Mohrenschildt had wed a Dorothy Pierson in Palm Beach County. Records would reveal that the marriage was short-lived but did produce a daughter named Alexandra de Mohrenschildt. Soon after the divorce, custody of the child had been granted to Nancy Tilton, who was Dorothy Pierson's sister.

Residence of Nancy Tilton

After his disappearance in Brussels, George had arrived in New York on March 15, 1977, and boarded a Greyhound bus to Palm Beach. He was to be a house guest of Nancy Tilton. She and her friend Katherine Loomis met him at the bus station the next day. He had no luggage and was carrying only a green attache case.

At the Tilton home, he was reunited with his daughter. The last 13 days of George de Mohrenschildt's life would be spent taking quiet solitary walks on the beach and reading in the privacy of his second floor bedroom.

CHAPTER TWENTY-FOUR

Records revealed that de Mohrenschildt had reached an agreement with <u>Reader's Digest</u> Editor Fulton Oursler, Jr., to do a four-day interview with writer Edward Epstein for an upcoming article. He would be compensated with a $4000 honorarium and the use of a Hertz rental car for four days. The two were to meet at the Breakers Hotel on Palm Beach on March 29, 1977. Epstein's research assistant, Nancy Lanoue, would also be in attendance.

When the day arrived, George awoke early. Lillian Romanic, the Tilton house cook, prepared his 7:30 breakfast of coffee and two slices of toast. It was a typical Spring day in South Florida. The sky was clear, and a gentle ocean breeze wafted across the compound. In addition to Romanic, the domestic staff consisted of housekeeper Anna Viisola and Coley Wimbley, who took care of the grounds.

Wimbley reported seeing George de Mohrenschildt crossing State Road A1A to the beach for a short walk and later being gone for a while in the blue rental car. By mid-morning, he had left for his morning interview appointment. By all accounts, the meeting went well. The three participants took a lunch break at Noon with the understanding that they would return by three o'clock to continue.

It's known that during those morning hours a staff investigator for the House Select Committee on Assassinations visited the Tilton home. Arriving from Miami, Gaeton Fonzi was met in the side yard by Alexandra de Mohrenschildt. He described her as being stunningly beautiful, with olive-toned skin and dark, piercing eyes.

Alexandra de Mohrenschildt

Fonzi identified himself and asked to speak with her father. She responded that he was in Palm Beach and she had no way to reach him. The investigator gave her his card and promised to return that evening. This brief encounter was to have a strange effect upon George.

When he returned to the Tilton home, he was said to have been in an upbeat mood. He was enjoying a light lunch of toast and coffee when Alexandra entered the room and informed him of the investigator's visit and that he would be back later that day. Records reveal that Lillian Romanic witnessed the exchange between de Mohrenschildt and his daughter but could not understand what was said because the two spoke in Spanish.

She could see that George was visibly disturbed by what Alexandra had told him. He sat looking at the identification card in his hand. After he left the kitchen and returned to his room on the second floor, de Mohrenschildt was seen by Anna Viisola lying quietly on his bed, staring straight at the ceiling.

Nancy Tilton was preparing to leave for an afternoon of playing bridge at the home of Mrs. Richard Knight. She had left instructions with the housekeeper to use a cassette tape recorder to record the afternoon's television soap opera programs so she could listen to them when she returned. The recorder was in her bedroom on the second floor. Alexandra de Mohrenschildt and Katheryn Loomis left at about 12:30 to shop for toilet supplies for George.

While Anna Viisola was doing her daily household cleaning on the second floor, George de Mohrenschildt left his bedroom and asked her about some strange noises he had heard while lying in his room. He said that the sounds appeared to be those of a cat that was scratching something.

Viisola assured George that no cat lived in the house and that he must be mistaken. She continued with her work. As she was going back downstairs, she reported, she saw de Mohrenschildt pacing back and forth in the upstairs hallway.

On that Tuesday afternoon - March 29, 1977 - Dianne and Laurie Tisdale were doing some painting in the upstairs apartment above the garage. Laurie was to move in once it had been refurbished. Coley Wimbley was working on the flower and shrub gardens that bordered the house.

Anna Viisola was busy cleaning downstairs. At around 1:30 P.M., she turned on the recorder for Nancy Tilton and then went to her private quarters, where she changed into a swimsuit to lie outside for a while. Lillian Romanic was also sunbathing in the back yard. So during those hours, there were five people either in the house or close to it at all times.

When Alexandra de Mohrenschildt returned, she asked Anna Viisola where her father might be. Told that he was likely still in his upstairs bedroom, Alexandra took the elevator to the second floor and then turned down the narrow hallway that led into a small sitting room.

There, she was confronted by the horrific sight of George de Mohrenschildt slumped over in a chair with blood pouring from his mouth and pooling at his feet. He was dressed in white slacks, a blue, long-sleeve turtleneck sweater and socks with no shoes.

His face was distorted, swollen and badly discolored. A double-barrel shotgun lay in a sideways position, across her father's left foot. Blood had splattered on the wall and baseboard. It was like a bizarre portrait frozen in time – motionless and absolutely silent.

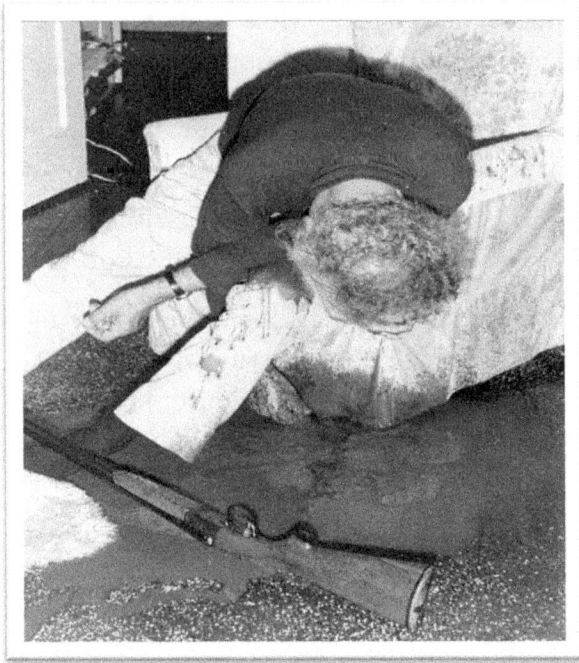

Emitting a scream of terror heard throughout the house, Alexandra rushed back to the elevator yelling that her father was dead. Quickly, a call was made to the Manalapan Police Department.

First on the scene was Patrolman Don McBride. Next came Palm Beach Sheriff's Office Detective Thomas Neighbors. The crime scene was secured, and photos and fingerprints were taken by Detective Gary Green. Neighbors would be the senior investigating officer.

Green searched de Mohrenschildt's room and found a brown attache case. Inside were numerous personal papers. One was a two-page personal affidavit, indicating that it was written on March 11, 1977, in Brussels, Belgium. It made reference to his friendship with Lee Harvey Oswald, the accused assassin of President John F. Kennedy.

In de Mohrenschildt's pants pocket, there was $379.70 in cash, along with a newspaper article from the March 20 edition of the <u>Dallas Morning News</u> reporting that George might possibly have been involved in or have knowledge of some type of conspiracy relative to the assassination. And Green found the business card that Gaeton Fonzi had left with Alexandra.

Realizing that the death of George de Mohrenschildt could be of major importance, the Sheriff's Office called in Detective John Skebe to supervise and assist in the investigation.

George's remains were removed from the Tilton home by Mike Bowden and Don Combs, from the Scobee-Combs Funeral Home in Boynton Beach. They were transported to the Bethesda Memorial Hospital morgue on March 30. The same day, an autopsy was performed by Palm Beach County Assistant Medical Examiner Dr. Gabino Cuevas, and cremation followed shortly thereafter.

All five of the individuals who were either in the Tilton home or on the grounds in close proximity were interviewed regarding their observations and recollections of that tragic afternoon.

Anna Viisola told investigators she never heard any type of gunshot or saw anything unusual. Coley Wimbley, who had been watering plants adjacent to the house, said the same thing. He was somewhat hard of hearing but his hearing aid had been in place. And none of the other three

– Lillian Romanic, Dianne Tisdale and Laurie Tisdale – reported noticing any sound that might have been a gunshot or any strange occurrences.

The weapon found at George de Mohrenschildt's feet was a 20-gauge Ithaca double barrel shotgun, bearing Serial Number 6114893. It belonged to Nancy Tilton and was stored in a small nightstand next to her bed with a box of Western Shot #9 shells. The gun had never been fired before.

Tilton's home was equipped with a security alarm system that would respond if any windows or doors were opened while it was set as "On Secure". If the system activated while the occupants were away, Rollins Protective Services would receive notification and in turn contact the Manalapan Police Department. In addition, a high-pitched beeping sound would be emitted if any window or door were to be opened. It was determined that during the morning and afternoon of March 29, 1977, the security alarm system had been in the "On Secure" mode.

Investigators found the cassette recorder in Nancy Tilton's second floor bedroom. And the tape was to provide an important clue. Playing it back, they could hear the television soap opera. But that was suddenly interrupted by an alarm from the security system.

Then, the beeping stopped - and it was followed by the sound of shoes walking on the hardwood flooring. Moments later, they heard a gun being fired. Because of that cassette tape recording, we know that George de Mohrenschildt died at 2:21 P.M. Eastern Standard Time. But the crime scene photos taken by Detective Gary Green clearly show him in a tall wingback chair with his clothes on and only black socks on his feet. No shoes can be seen next to his body or anywhere near it.

The authors located an individual who had listened to the cassette tape and confirmed that the footsteps were clearly identifiable as shoes on hardwood floors and that just moments after they stopped the gunshot was audible.

The Florida State Attorney's Office informed us that the original cassette tape has been destroyed. We also talked with an employee of Palm Beach County, who revealed that the George de Mohrenschildt case even today is sealed tight and that nothing concerning it can be found in the files.

Our attempt to get information from the Palm Beach County Sheriff's Office resulted in us being told that there is nothing on record or in their files – and that if there ever was, it would have been destroyed long ago.

CHAPTER TWENTY-FIVE

The de Mohrenschildt autopsy report seems to be consistent with a suicide, but it left some doubt and unanswered questions. The death scene photos showed clearly that there was no exit wound in George de Mohrenschildt's head, even though he supposedly had fired one barrel of the weapon into the roof of his mouth. The Palm Beach County Sheriff's Office processed the shotgun for the presence of latent prints. No fingerprints were found.

In light of the circumstances surrounding de Mohrenschildt's death, it's interesting to consider the layout and details of the Tilton home. It was a three-story structure that had four bedrooms on the second floor, along with a study, a bathroom and a small sitting room. The bedrooms were separated by a hallway that ran the length of the floor.

The Rollins system was wired to all of the first floor windows and doors and the second floor windows on the north end of the house, but not to the south-facing windows and those on the third floor. The sitting room where de Mohrenschildt's body was found had no windows but was connected through a doorway to Nancy Tilton's room. That was in the far southeastern portion of the floor, so her window was not included.

Whether self-inflicted or otherwise, the gruesome demise of George de Mohrenschildt remains, in some ways, a mystery. The Palm Beach County Sheriff's Office said they were 99% sure it was a suicide. But there's still a lingering possibility that something strange did in fact occur that afternoon on the second floor of the Tilton residence.

As things began to settle back down after de Mohrenschildt's death, Oltmans was contacted daily for interviews. He recorded in his notes that some proved to be very hurtful and annoying. Typical of those was one conducted by Wendle Rawls, Jr., of the <u>New York Times</u>. From the beginning, Rawls was most interested in how much Oltmans had made off of his story and how much money his family had. And he even went as far as to bring up Oltmans' personal life and his failed marriage that ended in 1960. Rawls was relentless, interrogating Willem on whether he was in Palm Beach to be interviewed by the <u>National Enquirer</u> for a large payment.

It had become a familiar pattern of questioning. By now accustomed to these attacks on his character, Oltmans fired back that he was a freelance journalist that investigated stories and then revealed his findings, and that's how he made his living. He pointed out that other freelancers earned their money the same way, but they were never asked that type of question.

And he asked Rawls, "How on earth does the amount of money my family has in their private bank account have anything to do with my investigation of President Kennedy's assassination or the investigation of George de Mohrenschildt?" Fnally came the moment that brought the interview to an end. Looking Oltmans right in the eyes, Rawls said, "This question will most likely make you very uneasy and upset, but I must ask it. Are you a homosexual?"

Willem stared right back at him and replied, "So you even want to go behind my bedroom door." And then he said, "Maybe you should call my friend Peter Van de Wouw in London."

Oltmans recorded in his notes that he did everything he could to remain professional and civil, but he was quite obviously hurt and angry. The questions had been mean and cruel and had nothing to do with Oltmans' findings during his ten-year investigation and friendship with George de Mohrenschildt.

On April 11, 1977, the <u>New York Times</u> published Rawls' article, and it referred to the Dutch journalist as a showman who was unreliable and had questionable motives. The damaging story would be read by millions, so there was nothing left for the Dutchman to do except to pick up the pieces of what was left of his journalist career and move on, trying to maintain some level of respect and honor.

But the discrediting of Willem Oltmans wouldn't stop there. Shortly after that article was published, a story appeared in the <u>Algemeen Dagblad</u> (AD), a newspaper in Rotterdam, The Netherlands, with a circulation of 315,000 readers daily. Peter Hammecourt wrote, "With Willem Oltmans, you never know when his true facts stop and his fantasies begin."

The article was filled with negative statements about Oltmans. He recorded in his notes that he had never even heard of Hammecourt. It had become quite clear that even journalists from his home country were out to discredit him and cast doubt on his work. He was now the target of a steady stream of attempted ridicule.

Next came AVRO Television of The Netherlands. They told viewers never to listen to or believe any story the reporter Willem Oltmans told. In his notes, Willem recorded that any of the journalists that worked for AVRO Television or the AD would have been front and center had they had an opportunity to break the George de Mohrenschildt story.

Oltmans knew deep inside that his motives were professional and he had a clear objective to investigate the facts behind the assassination of President Kennedy and what role de Mohrenschildt had played. But the constant campaign to discredit him was painful nonetheless.

In the end, Oltmans came to believe that the whole debacle boiled down to journalistic jealousy and animosity and a concerted effort by the Dutch Government to discredit his work. And in the year 2000, that would be proven in a court of law to be true.

Just as he was ready to wash his hands of the whole de Mohrenschildt affair, Willem Oltmans received a mysterious phone call at his Amsterdam apartment. It was from a man identifying himself as Jim Adams.

He told Oltmans that he was interested in producing an epic film concerning the assassination of President John F. Kennedy. Having seen Oltmans on news reports concerning his own investigation, he felt that the two of them should get together and discuss the project.

A meeting was set for May 31, 1977, at the Amsterdam Marriott Hotel. Willem's notes revealed that he was very suspicious of this "Jim Adams" and discussed the upcoming encounter with Carel Enkelaar at the headquarters of NOS Television. Reluctant to become involved any further with the subject, Oltmans at first considered calling the meeting off. But after several days of pondering his next move, he decided to go ahead.

CHAPTER TWENTY-SIX

Upon his arrival at Room 437 at the Marriott, Willem was met by a middle-aged man with dark hair and a very heavy accent. As the two men sat talking, "Jim Adams" revealed his real identity as General Donald A. Donaldson. Totally shocked by this disclosure, Oltmans listened intently as Donaldson spoke of his early years in the military.

He was originally from Bulgaria, and his Bulgarian name at birth was Dimiter Adamov Dimitrov (Deko). He had been a member of the resistance movement against the Nazis in World War II and part of the Democratic Liberation Movement in 1943. Fearing a communist takeover, he fled to the United States. President Franklin Roosevelt had declared him a United States citizen, given him the name "Donald A. Donaldson" and made him a titular general.

Dimiter Adamov Dimitrov, AKA:
General Donald A. Donaldson

As Donaldson was speaking, Oltmans studied him cautiously. "My friends at the Pentagon know all about this meeting here," the general said. "You showed great courage bringing out the details of George de Mohrenschildt's involvement in the conspiracy in President Kennedy's murder. You know you were completely right. George de Mohrenschildt was one of the key participants. Do you realize the danger you've been in since you made your findings public?"

Donaldson went on to say that de Mohrenschildt had asked the wrong people for immunity. "If he had only gone to the right people, his death could have been avoided," he declared. "Going to the Soviets in Brussels was not a good move."

Next, Donaldson told Oltmans that de Mohrenschildt, upon his return to the United States, had gone straight to Washington. That also was not wise, Donaldson said. While there, de Mohrenschildt had been offered safe passage to Mexico if he would sign a document prepared by the CIA. He did so and was directed to go to Florida.

And then, after a short time there and subsequent to his meeting with Edward Epstein, he was murdered by two men, according to Donaldson. Willem took note of Donaldson's cold and calculating stare as he described the killers entering the Tilton home undetected during the time that George was being interviewed in Palm Beach.

He said that they had waited on the second floor in order to ambush him upon his return. And having killed him, they were able to slip out of the house as easily as they had entered. It had been an execution plan from start to finish, made to look like a suicide and carried out with such stealth that no one nearby heard or saw anything.

Here, we would like to offer our own speculation regarding the chain of events. We believe that the two men surprised de Mohrenschildt. They first struck him in the mouth area, causing a fracture of the jaw, which is confirmed in the autopsy report. Then, the Tilton 20-gauge was pushed into de Mohrenschildt's mouth, with both barrels wrapped in a homemade silencer to muffle the sound of the blast.

One barrel of the shotgun was fired, at an upward angle. The mortally-wounded de Mohrenschildt was pushed back in the wingback chair, and the weapon was placed at his feet. But the blood splatter on the wall behind the chair and to its sides was low - around the baseboard area. Investigators on the scene mentioned that they found that concerning.

And there was no exit wound. Furthermore, fingerprints were never found on the shotgun. Death scene photos show no blood on the ends of its barrels. And, of course, none of the five people in and around the Tilton house at the time heard a gunshot.

Records in the Robert Cutler Collection stored at Baylor University reveal that Edward Epstein's interview history was plagued by bizarre coincidences. After a planned meeting with Epstein, former FBI third-in-command William Sullivan had met his death under suspicious circumstances.

Epstein had arranged for an interview with Frances Gary Powers, but the former U2 pilot was killed in a strange helicopter crash shortly thereafter. And de Mohrenschildt's lifeless body had been discovered shortly after the two had spent a couple of hours together. In Willem Oltmans' archives, we found a note in which he referred to Edward Epstein as "straight CIA".

As this first meeting with Donaldson came to an end, Oltmans recorded that he was completely shocked by what he had been told. "Could this all be real?" he wrote. "Was this whole thing nothing but a mere plot to discredit me even more?" He feared that revealing the new twist would cause a total disaster by making his initial findings appear even less truthful, now that he had yet another sensational story to tell the world.

After carefully considering the downsides, Oltmans decided to proceed with caution but keep these new allegations confidential until the moment was right. Landing the George de Mohrenschildt story was already big, but if General Donaldson's claims proved to be true, it could end up being one of the most monumental news stories of Oltmans' long journalistic career.

After returning to his apartment that evening, Willem Oltmans wrote of his excitement regarded this new development but also noted his apprehension that this General Donaldson might have been sent to plant a wild story that could never be proven and would leave Oltmans open to ridicule once again and possibly even be the death knell of his career as a journalist.

In the next meeting with General Donaldson at the same Marriott Hotel, he told Oltmans of his plans for the film about the Kennedy assassination. As he talked of costs that might exceed 20 million dollars and mentioned that his company, Deko Productions, would need financial help, Oltmans began to see the direction the conversation was taking.

When Donaldson finally asked if there was someone among his contacts around the world who would lend him 50 thousand dollars, Willem quickly responded that he didn't have friends like that and he would have to find his financing somewhere else.

After that blatant request for money, the meeting went on and Donaldson began to praise Oltmans for his courage in taking on such a sensitive case. He even went so far as to call Willem his hero. Quickly switching gears, Donaldson asked, "Did you know that Jackie Kennedy received a full report on who really killed her husband?" He also stated that President Gerald Ford was aware that there were five bullets fired at John Kennedy that day in Dealey Plaza.

Donaldson warned Oltmans that if and when he returned to the United States he would have to remain constantly on guard because he now would be a prime target of the people involved in the plot. And they would not hesitate for a moment to eliminate him as they had others who got too close to unraveling the truth behind the assassination.

As this meeting drew to a close, he tried to strike a bargain with Oltmans. Donaldson offered to release all the names of the individuals that were involved in President Kennedy's assassination and to identify who gave the direct order to carry it out, under one condition. Willem would have to go to Washington and arrange a personal meeting between him and President Jimmy Carter.

Oltmans couldn't believe what he was hearing. This man would release to him the facts behind the killing, but only if he could arrange a face-to-face meeting at the White House with the current President? Annoyed by this strange request, he sternly told Donaldson to stop playing games and to give him the names - if he indeed did know who was behind President Kennedy's murder.

Suddenly, Donaldson leaped to his feet and rushed over to his opened suitcase on the bed stand. He pulled out a .38-caliber revolver and charged Oltmans with it cocked and loaded. Placing the gun under Willem's chin with the barrel at point blank range, Donaldson warned, "I will shoot and kill you and go to prison for the rest of my life if you ever reveal anything I have told you to anyone but President Carter."

Oltmans later recorded in his notes that, with the weapon still pushing upward against his skin, he thought hard and offered Donaldson the opportunity to go to the NOS Television studios and tell his story on film to be broadcast throughout the world - and that NOS Television was prepared to pay him $100,000 to do so. That relieved the tension, and as his temper cooled, Donaldson backed away and once again praised Oltmans for being a man of courage.

A great feeling of relief swept over Willem as he left the hotel room. Later, back at his apartment, he would recall a similar incident, when he had met with Glenn Bryan Smith at the Hotel Terminus in Utrecht, The Netherlands. On that occasion, he had been threatened with being thrown out of a airplane miles out over the Atlantic Ocean if he didn't end his investigation of George de Mohrenschildt.

Being an investigative journalist surely had its drawbacks and scary moments, as Oltmans had learned during his long career. Bodily harm or even death could be waiting around any corner.

CHAPTER TWENTY-SEVEN

Sitting there alone, he considered what he should do concerning General Donald Donaldson. The man's claims seemed far-fetched and almost unbelievable. The fact that he had asked for $50,000 seemed very strange and outrageous to Oltmans and made him skeptical that his statements regarding his possession of inside information concerning President Kennedy's assassination were true.

After weighing his options, Oltmans decided to ignore Donaldson's threats and to reveal his findings and this new witness who claimed to have pertinent information concerning the murder and conspiracy. Specifically, he would release everything he had been told and Donaldson's name to the United States Justice Department and to the House Select Committee on Assassinations. In addition, he would appear on ABC's "Good Morning America" and tell all he knew. And, finally, that would bring Willem Oltmans' long investigation into President Kennedy's assassination to an end.

A closer look at Dimiter Adamov Dimitrov (Deko) reveals an individual who was well known to the United States State Department, the Central Intelligence Agency and the FBI and used many aliases such as Lyle Kelly, James Allen and Donald Donaldson.

Records would reveal that Dimitrov was used as a subject in what would become known as the Artichoke Project. Subjects were confined and drugged, and electric shock treatments were administered. While being held in a military prison in Panama, Dimitrov claimed, he had met individuals who passed on secret information including names of those involved in President John F. Kennedy's assassination.

On September 8, 1977, Oltmans went before ABC cameras and made a fourteen-minute presentation of his latest findings. And of course they were met with skepticism on all sides. Most major news outlets never even aired the new Oltmans story. The House Select Committee accepted the new information and thanked Oltmans for his work but never found anything credible in the new allegations.

In the end, a somber Willem Oltmans told Robert Tanenbaum that he had done all he could do to help the committee and it was now time for their own investigators to take over. Feeling defeated, Oltmans declared, "I wash my hands of the whole thing. It's yours now. I have given you all I found during my ten-year investigation concerning President Kennedy's assassination and all that was revealed to me by George de Mohrenschildt. I now return to my home in The Netherlands knowing I that told the truth."

And with those words, Willem Oltmans' long struggle to share what he knew with the world came to an end. As he exited Robert Tanenbaum's office and got into a waiting taxi, he was met by no one - no cameras flashing, no microphones being pushed at him. In the end, he had become simply another face on a busy sidewalk in Washington, D. C.

Oltmans found his thoughts going back to the time just six months ago when he had to wade through crowds of reporters as he exited the Rayburn Building. He took a last look out the rear window of the taxi as it sped into traffic, recalling how the American mainstream media had discredited him and smeared his investigation and him personally until everything he had done to reveal the true story concerning George de Mohrenschildt and the Kennedy assassination was simply washed away.

But it was now all behind him. He sank back into his seat, now just one more anonymous person passing by the capital's iconic buildings, unaware of the many secrets they might be protecting. What a story he had uncovered. What a story he had told.

After he returned to The Netherlands to continue his journalistic career, Oltmans would continue to become involved in controversial issues right to the end. By the late 1980s, he had developed a large global network of contacts with whom he planned to work as a consultant, introducing them to Eastern European business opportunities. Sadly, this venture would fail, leaving Oltmans disillusioned and bitter. Looking for a new direction, he moved to South Africa in 1990. His two brothers had settled there permanently years earlier, and joining them in doing so seemed like a good choice.

Within two years, Oltmans had once again intervened in local politics – thereby angering many in the South African government. On August 17, 1992, he was charged with espionage and deported. In his notes, Oltmans wrote that he felt confident that the Dutch security system was behind the action.

Back in The Netherlands, he finally won his long, drawn-out legal battle and obtained a significant financial judgment against the Dutch Government. He moved into a penthouse apartment in the canal district at the heart of Amsterdam, where he expected to live out his last days at ease with his new-found wealth and his journalistic integrity restored.

In 2004, Willem Oltmans would be diagnosed with incurable liver cancer. He struggled for months with failing health, working to secure his archives and making arrangements for his memoirs to be published. On September 30, at age 79, he died in the privacy of his penthouse, surrounded by close friends and with his lifelong partner Peter Van de Wouw at his side.

But as was his nature, he had planned each and every detail of his own passing. Rather than waiting to succumb to the disease, Oltmans opted for euthanasia, using the services of The Right To Die Society of The Netherlands, which since 1973 has helped terminally ill individuals to end their own lives in a peaceful, controlled setting.

He chose his final resting place beside his parents in the "Den en Rust" (Pine and Rest) cemetery in Belthoven. While in The Netherlands, the authors visited the family grave site, which is a small, peaceful plot nestled in a quiet forest with slate stone walkways.

As we stood next to Willem's grave, a light rain began to fall, and in the stillness of the forest all that could be heard was the swaying of the pines and the gentle sound of the raindrops. The long and controversial life of one of the most famous Dutchmen of modern times had ended. But before it did, Willem Oltmans regained that which was most valuable to him: his credibility as a journalist.

And he had never failed to live up to the one overriding standard that he had set for himself: the real truth must come out and be told, no matter what the consequences.

CHAPTER TWENTY-EIGHT

The authors found during their research for this book overwhelming, convincing evidence in Willem Oltmans' personal archives that he was first and foremost an honest, professional journalist.

The meticulous note-taking that he had done for his entire life beginning at age nine made it possible for us to follow a day-to-day chronology of the close and intimate personal friendship between him and George de Mohrenschildt. Those notes revealed de Mohrenschildt's overwhelming feelings of guilt for his direct influence over Lee Harvey Oswald and the murder of President John F. Kennedy.

And they included the stunning confession from George de Mohrenschildt that he had in fact guided and instructed Lee Harvey Oswald on how the assassination could be carried out.

Shortly before his death, Oltmans bequeathed all of his notes and his massive collection of bound personal diaries covering his long journalistic career to the Royal Dutch Library in Den Haag, The Netherlands. He hoped that by preserving his investigative work he would make it possible for researchers and scholars in later years to look into the past and see the hidden facts behind the crime of the century.

With the help of the Special Collections Department staff and Dr. Ad Leerinvelt of the Royal Dutch Library, we were able to follow Willem Oltmans' carefully-preserved paper trail, and piece together this fascinating true story and bring it to print.

Sadly, the discrediting and smear tactics used by Dutch Minister of Foreign Affairs Joseph Luns to sow suspicion regarding Oltmans' honesty

– along with the campaign by the mainstream media in the United States to cast doubt on his work and his integrity - would greatly diminish any impact that his investigation might have had on confirming (1) whether or not George de Mohrenschildt was an influencing force on Lee Harvey Oswald and (2) who was really behind the assassination of President Kennedy.

With the passage of time, that fateful Friday afternoon in Dallas has faded into distant memory. And many of the details regarding what transpired in the months leading up to November 22, 1963, have remained – for the most part – hidden in the shadows. Grainy old newsreels, yellowed newspaper headlines and faded pages are just about all that is left now.

Many thousands of sealed documents concerning President Kennedy's assassination have been labeled TOP SECRET and kept from the American people, we are told, for reasons of National Security. Time seems to have dampened the passion that once fueled Americans' search for the truth.

In the final months of Willem Oltmans' life, he reached out and secured a safe and secure place to store and archive his years and years of note-taking, letters and files, diaries and documentation of his investigative journalist work. It was his fervent hope that eventually someone would step forward and take a second look at his carefully-detailed records. The authors have done that, and all of our findings are presented here for your consideration in OLTMANS: *A Moment In History.*

"The truth lies before us. Let none of us fail to set history right out of fear to seek the truth."

-- Tommy Wilkens & Hilde Wilkens Vanrenterghem

Epilogue

Finally, this book is an up-close look at journalist Willem Oltmans' life and the intimate friendship that revealed the secret and private lives of George and Jeanne de Mohrenschildt and their involvement with Lee Harvey Oswald and the assassination of President John F. Kennedy.

It is clear beyond any doubt that George de Mohrenschildt had intelligence connections with more than one government and in fact was possibly associated with at least three different government intelligence agencies around the world during his life.

Documents declassified in recent years have shown that George de Mohrenschildt's Central Intelligence Agency file contained several reports submitted by him to the agency on topics concerning Yugoslavia. A large portion of his personal file is still classified as SECRET.

As more and more records and documents are declassified and released through the Freedom of Information Act and private researchers' diligence in searching for the facts, the once blurry picture of what at first appeared to be a teacher/businessman and his wife caught up by coincidence in the assassination of a President has begun to come into focus.

Since de Mohrenschildt's death, nearly forty years ago as of this writing, it has been revealed that CIA operative J. Walton Moore was the individual who gave de Mohrenschildt the go-ahead and sanctioned the meeting with Lee Harvey Oswald. We also know through the Oltmans archives that Moore and de Mohrenschildt had an ongoing friendship and that Moore on at least four occasions was a dinner guest at the de Mohrenschildt home. Both George and Jeanne were on a first-name basis with Moore.

And the personal correspondence with former director of the CIA George H. W. Bush leaves little if any doubt that George de Mohrenschildt was an operative for that agency. A declassified CIA file from 1976 confirms the fact that George de Mohrenschildt had been used as a source for foreign intelligence. He was considered by many to be brutal and dangerous and was involved in several clandestine operations in the Caribbean and Central America during the 1960s.

His involvement in Haiti, the tiny, corrupt island nation only a few short miles off the coast of Cuba, is well-documented, and his close dealings with the Haitian dictator Francois "Papa Doc" Duvalier are still shrouded in mystery and intrigue.

It's believed by many that de Mohrenschildt was positioned on the island by the U. S. Central Intelligence Agency to set up a *coup d'etat* that would take down the Duvalier government and replace it with a new hand-picked leader - a shrewd Haitian politician/banker by the name of Clemard Joseph Charles. He was the president and principle shareholder of the Bank Commercial of Port-au-Prince.

Records reveal that on May 7, 1963, George and Jeanne de Mohrenschildt and Clemard Joseph Charles attended a meeting in Washington, D.C., at the office of the United States Army Chief of Staff for Intelligence. Coordinating this meeting was the assistant Director of the Office of Intelligence of the U.S. Army, Dorothe K. Matlack. Also in attendance was Tony Czaikowski of the Central Intelligence Agency.

Documents now available show that during this meeting Clemard Joseph Charles, with George de Mohrenschildt sitting by his side, had asked that the United States Marine Corps be sent into Haiti to attack and overthrow the Duvalier government.

Years later, when interviewed by the House Select Committee on Assassinations, Dorothe Matlack would testify that it was her understanding during the meeting that George de Mohrenschildt was in charge and was in some ways leading Clemard Joseph Charles. She went on to disclose that she found George de Mohrenschildt to be a very disturbing individual.

The Oltmans archives outlined George de Mohrenschildt's private world in great detail. A clear picture soon emerges of an individual who was a true master of deception. He lived his life on many levels and had a number of identities that could never be tied or even traced to him.

Recently released records show that as early as 1954, de Mohrenschildt had a close connection with the former head of Radio Free Europe and the eventual chief and director of the Central Intelligence Agency, Allen Dulles.

A CIA agent by the name of Herbert Itkin mentioned in his notes that Dulles had introduced a person by the name of Philip Harbin to him. He would later admit that the man he had met was really George de Mohrenschildt. And the name "Harbin" was an interesting choice. George's wife Jeanne was born in Harbin, China.

He was a master of multiple personalities and a seasoned undercover intelligence operative who could create an unbreakable cover story for almost any situation. He always stayed two steps ahead and played his role in the shadows. Denial of involvement was his standard response.

George de Mohrenschildt was a highly-polished intellectual, living his complex life as almost a James Bond-type figure. He had a reputation as a womanizer with bisexual tendencies. Traveling the world ostensibly as an international oil geologist/businessman/stamp collector allowed de Mohrenschildt entry into some of the most dangerous places in the world. Records of his ventures would show a pattern that placed him in cities and countries just before a coup or an invasion was about to occur.

In Guatemala, de Mohrenschildt showed up on foot at a Cuban exile training camp a day prior to the Bay of Pigs invasion. His presence in Haiti as a coup was being plotted was passed off as a mere coincidence. But de Mohrenschildt was likely used by the Central Intelligence Agency in Iran, Egypt, Indonesia, Panama, Guatemala, Haiti, Nicaragua and Pakistan.

In the course of Willem Oltmans' investigation, he soon began to recognize that these strange coincidences were anything but that. Slowly and methodically over the years of their intimate friendship, he would continue to work his investigative journalist skills with de Mohrenschildt and always turn the conversation back to his relationship with Lee Oswald - letting him reveal the details as slowly as he liked.

In a newly-released FBI document (# 89-43, filed by the Dallas Office on April 19,1977). Jeanne de Mohrenschildt told Special Agents Udo H. Specht and Lloyd B. Harrell, Jr., that at no time during the de Mohrenschildts' more than ten years of friendship with Willem Oltmans had he ever pressured her or George in any way concerning Lee Oswald or the John Kennedy assassination.

Everything that was told to Oltmans in his conversations with George and Jeanne de Mohrenschildts was later recorded in his notes and diaries. He never left to chance the possibility that something important that was said would slip by or be forgotten.

And from these archives of Oltmans' recollections, we're able to see the mindset of the couple before and after the assassination of President Kennedy and George's self-confessed involvement and mentoring of Lee Harvey Oswald in the months leading up to it. One of George de Mohrenschildt's closest friends from the Dallas White Russian community, George Bouhe, once said that The Baron was better equipped than anyone to have talked about the event.

As with other major historical events that remain shrouded in controversy, all of the facts behind the assassination may never be revealed. Time marches on, people pass away and the fear of involvement causes many to take their secrets to the grave.

A virtual industry of JFK assassination conspiracy theories, misinformation, and related articles, books and movies has developed since 1963, making it much harder for anyone to discern the real facts.

But a well-preserved archive like that of Willem Oltmans, with its meticulously-documented investigative work, gives us a window into his life and how his involvement came about due to that chance airport meeting with Marguerite Oswald and the incredible mental powers of "The Amazing Dutchman", Gerard Croiset. Without Oltmans' records and his private friendship with George de Mohrenschildt, the story of the close relationship between "The Baron" and Lee Harvey Oswald in the months leading up to President Kennedy's assassination would have either been lost to history or passed off as mere happenstance. But thanks to Willem Oltmans, the truth can once and for all be revealed in this book.

As some who knew him have said, an old Russian proverb might apply perfectly to the mysterious George de Mohrenschildt:

"The soul of the other person is in the darkness".

The End

Sources And Discovery

The Willem Oltmans Archives Dutch Royal Library, Den Haag, The Netherlands:

Willem Oltmans private personal diaries/personal notes

Oltmans Personal Diary 1964 I – Denver, Dallas

Oltmans Personal Diary 1967 I – New York, Dallas – Pages 3275 through 3283

Oltmans Personal Diary 1967 XX – Dallas – Pages 8398 through 8422

Oltmans Personal Diary 1977 I - New York, Kentucky

Oltmans Personal Diary 1977 II – Miami, Houston – Pages 0108 through 0290

Oltmans Personal Diary 1977 III – Pages 0300 through 0434

Oltmans Personal Diary 1977 IV – New York – Pages 0449 through 0490

Oltmans Personal Diary 1977 V – London – Pages 9169 through 9179

Oltmans Personal Diary 1977 VI - Pages 9180 through 9223

Oltmans Personal Diary 1977 VII – Dallas -- Pages 9645 through 9723

EEN REPORTAGE OVER DE KENNEDY-MOORDENAARS – Willem Oltmans, A.W.Bruna & Zoon Utrecht/Antwerpen 1977

Memoires 1967-1968 (Memoires Willem Oltmans) Pages 257-260, Pages 277-278, Pages 284-285, Papieren Tyger, Breda

Memoires 1970-1971 (Memoires Willem Oltmans) Pages 205-206, Papieren Tyger, Breda

Memoires 1968-1970 (Memoires Willem Oltmans) Pages 93-94, Pages 101-118, Pages 188-192, Pages 203-204, Pages 208-211, Pages 298-299, Papiereh Tyger, Breda

Memoires 1972-1973 (Memoires Willem Oltmans) Pages 243-320, Papiereh Tyger, Breda

Memoires 1976-1977 (Memoires Willem Oltmans), Papieren Tyger, Breda

Steven Martin (Memories of Marguerite Oswald)

House Select Committee on Assassinations Official Final Report (Oltmans Testimony)

Palm Beach County Sheriff's Office (Official Crime Scene Investigation Report) dated 3-29-1977 Case Number #77-11753)

National Archives (JFK Assassination Records Pertaining to George de Mohrenschildt):

File #80T01357A, Record #104-10166-10266

File #80T01357A, Record #104-10166-10268

File # 80T01357A, Record #104-10166-10269

File #80T01357A, Record # 104-10166-10270

File # 80T01357A, Record # 104-10166-10271

Unpublished Manuscript by George de Mohrenschildt (I Am A Patsy, I Am A Patsy)

James Richards - Queensland, Australia (Credit for de Mohrenschildt death scene photo)

The Mary Ferrell Foundation (Willem Oltmans & George de Mohrenschildt Files)

Perry Vermeulen (Lee Harvey Oswald Via Rotterdam naar Dallas – moord op JFK)

Author/Poet Paul Foreman

Jack Harrison Pollack (<u>Croiset, the Clairvoyant,</u> Published 1964 Doubleday)

Joan Mellon (<u>Our Man In Haiti</u>)

Robert Cutler Collection Baylor University

<u>Gallery Magazine,</u> April 1978 ("The Missing General" by Willem Oltmans)

Den en Rust Begraafplaats en Crematorium, Bilthoven, The Netherlands

Mijn Vriend Surkano (Willem Oltmans)

Indonesia Diobok-Obok (Willem Oltmans)

Alphabetical Index

www.ingramcontent.com/pod-product-compliance
Lightning Source LLC
La Vergne TN
LVHW051630080426
835511LV00016B/2267